Japan
Coloring Book

Adult Colouring Books

Aryla Publishing 2020

978-1-912675-76-0

www.arylapublishing.com

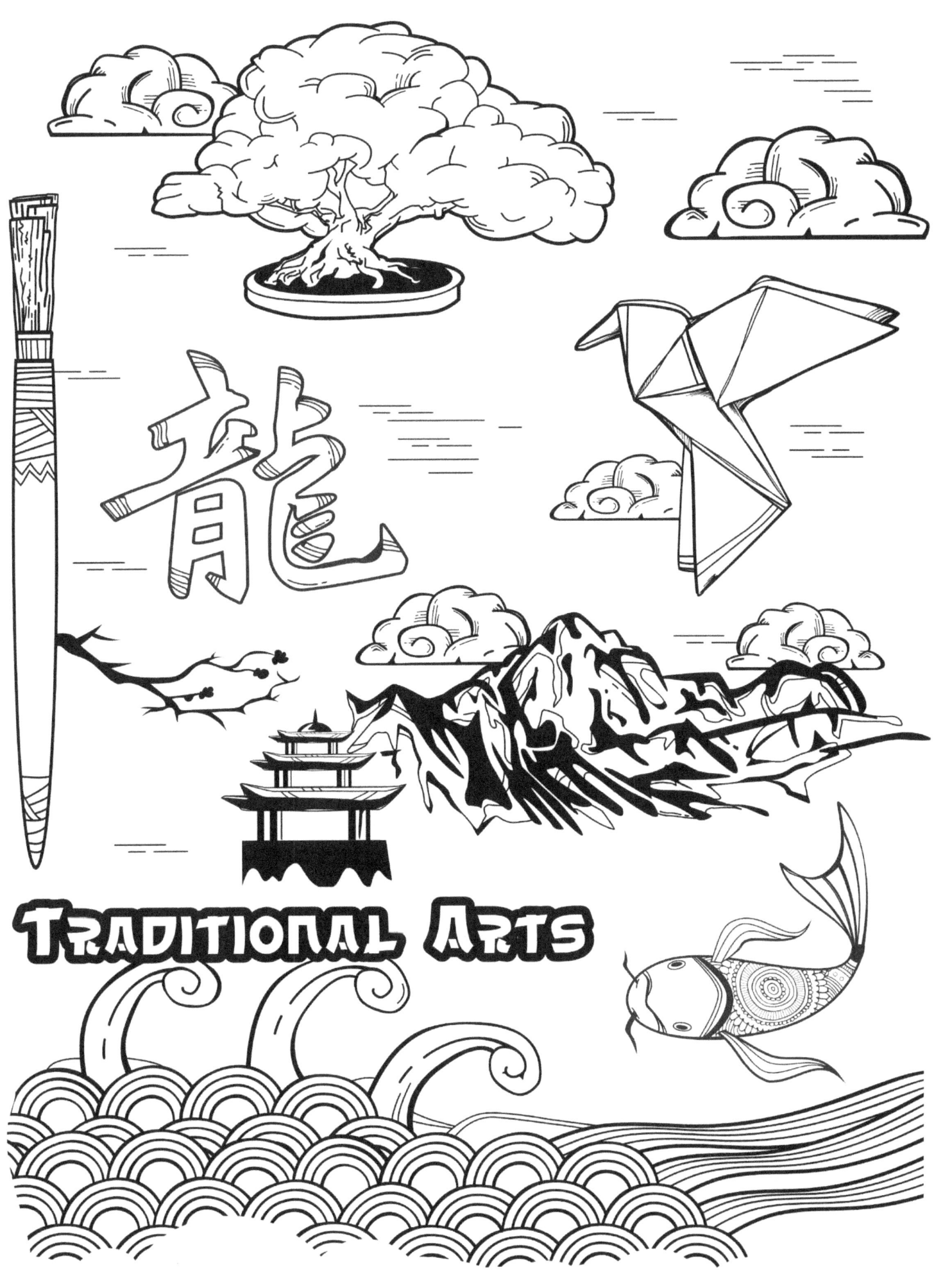

TRADITIONAL ARTS

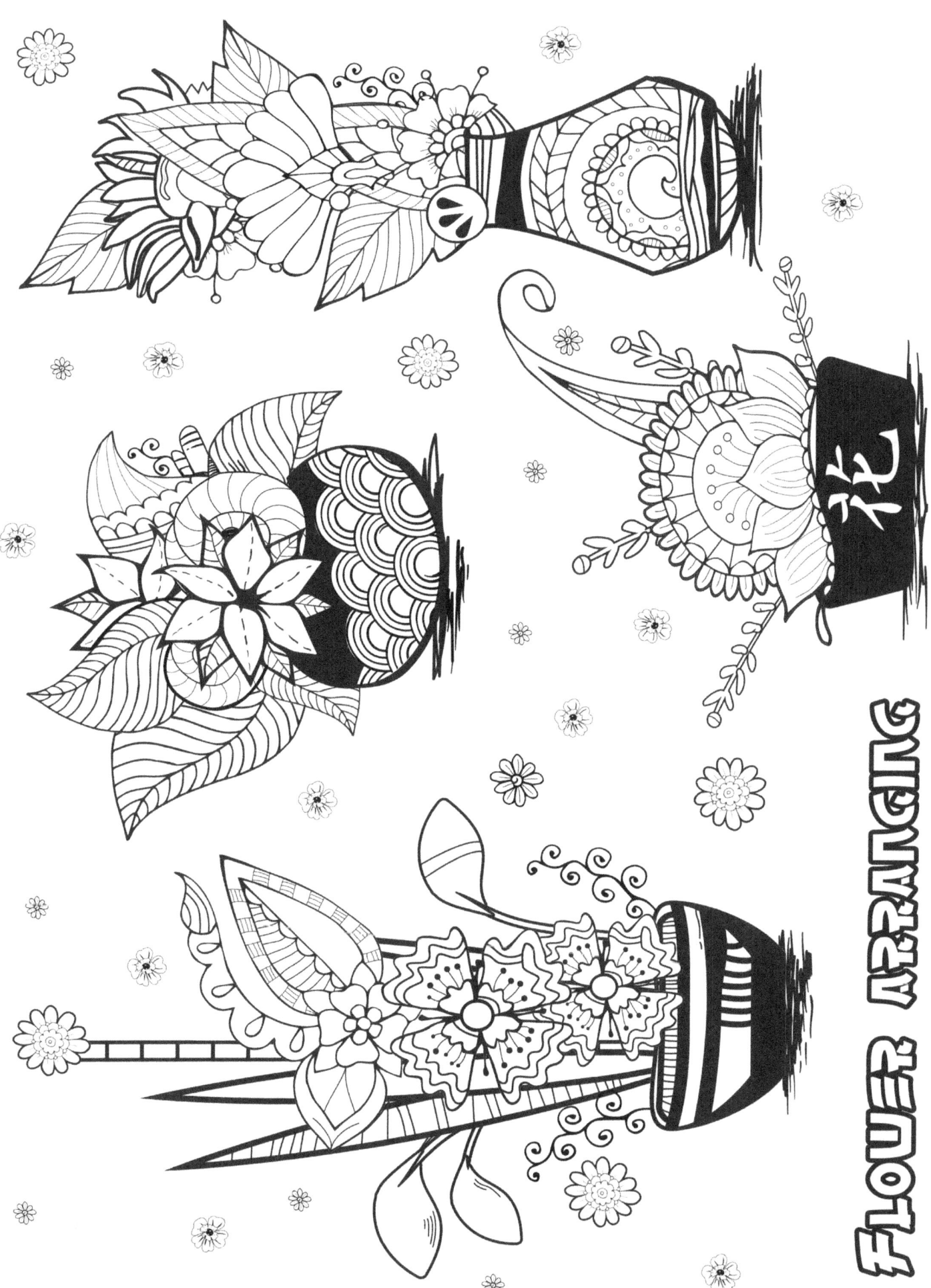

FLOWER ARRANGING

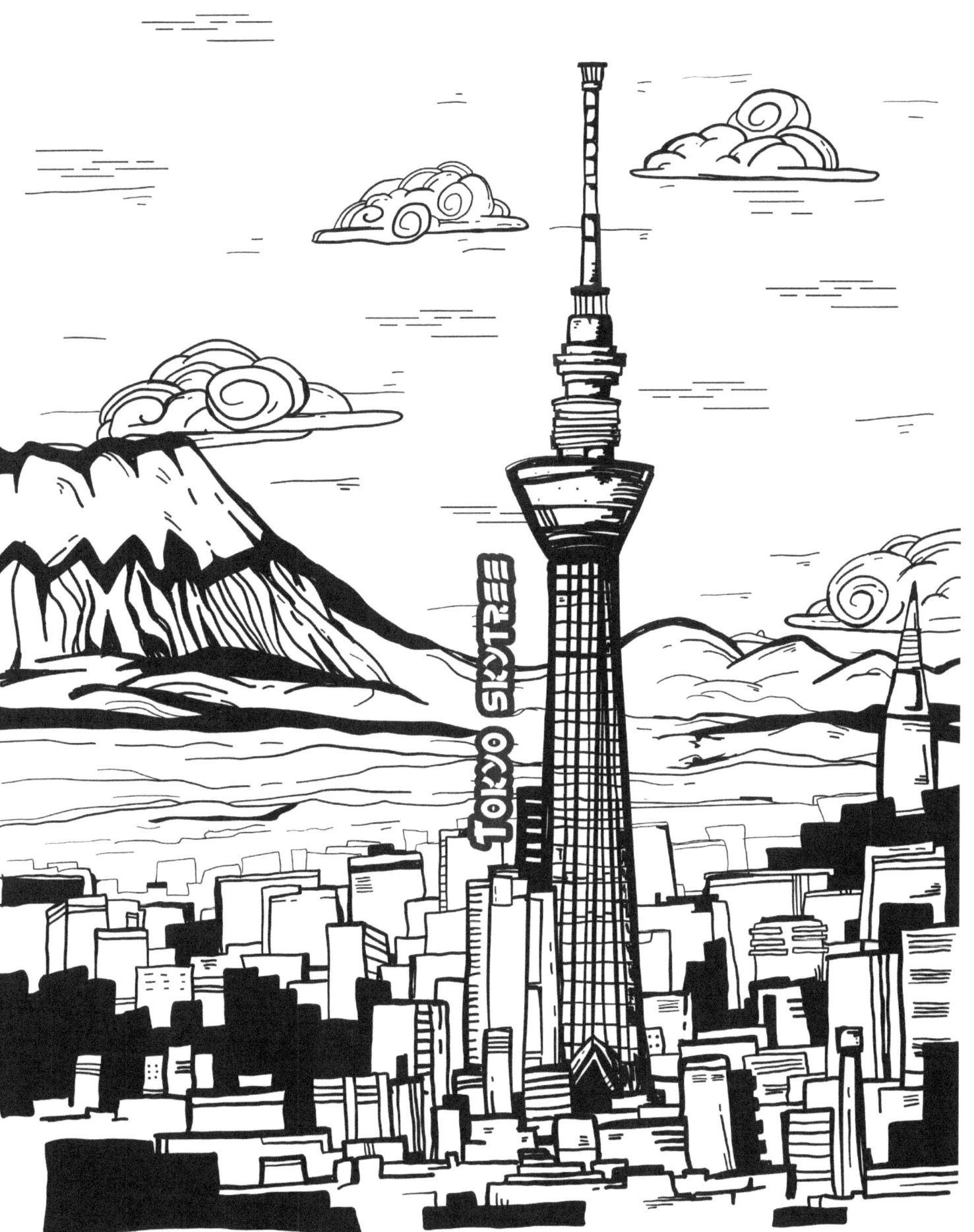

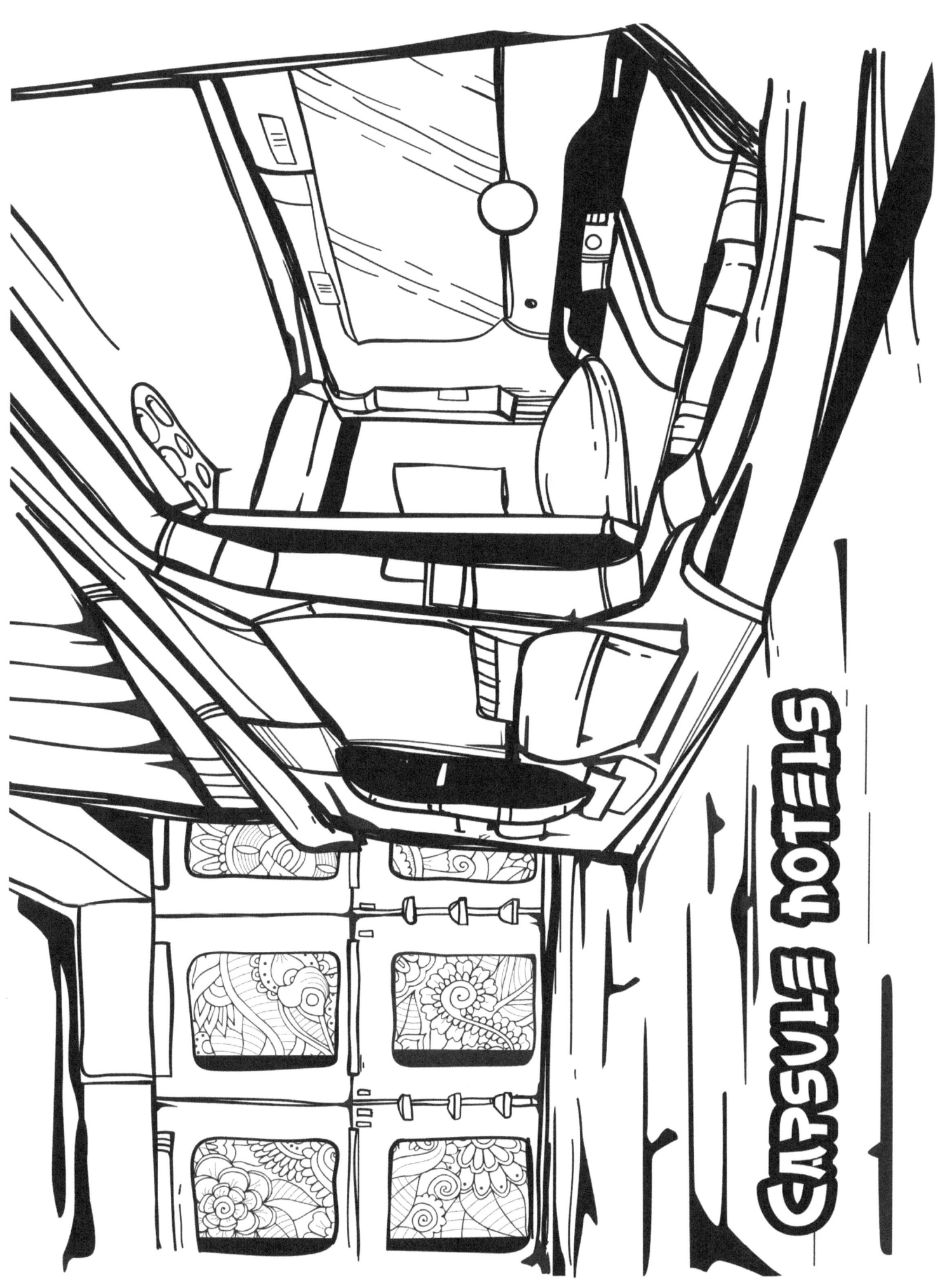

CAPSULE HOTELS

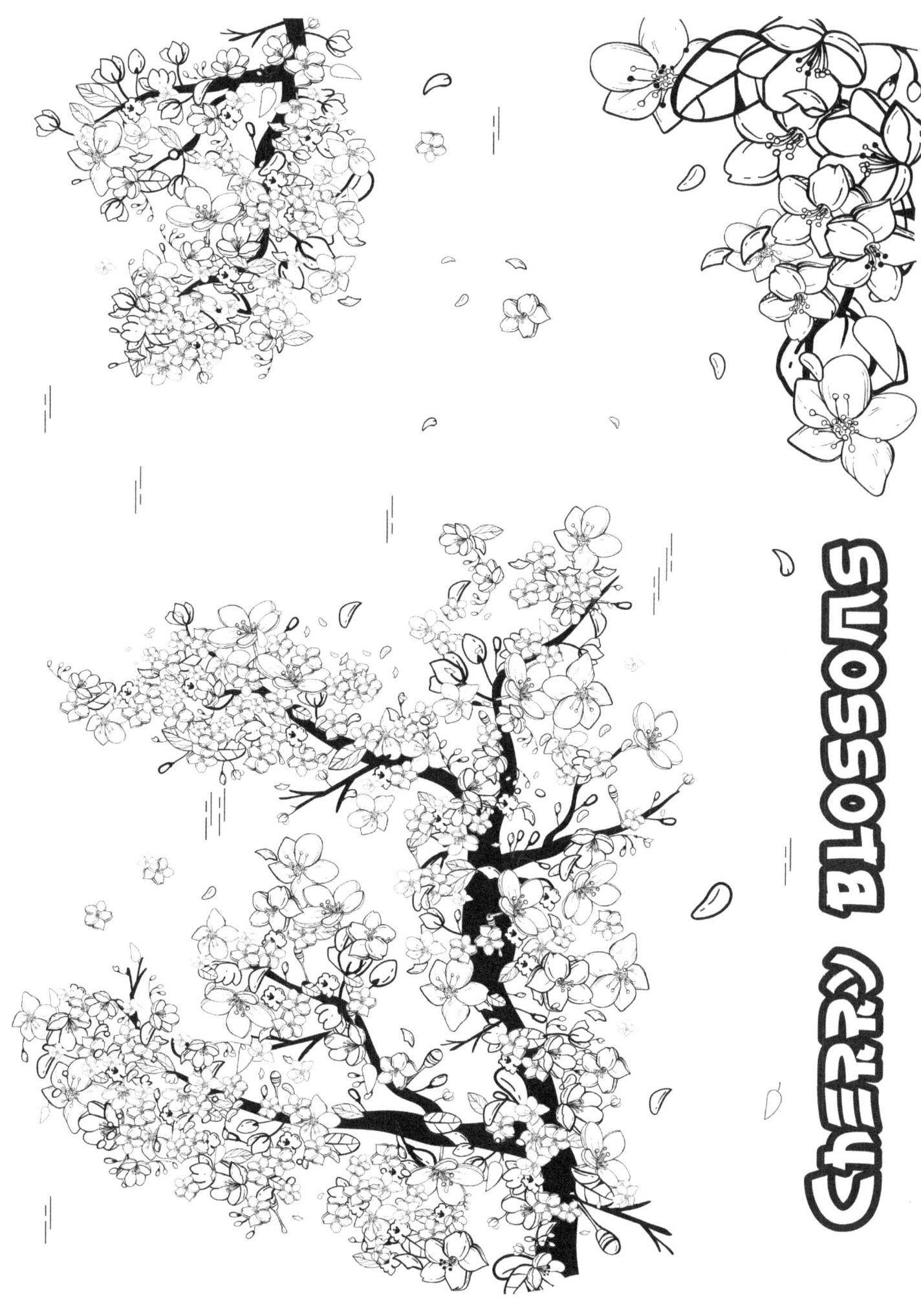

CHERRY BLOSSOMS

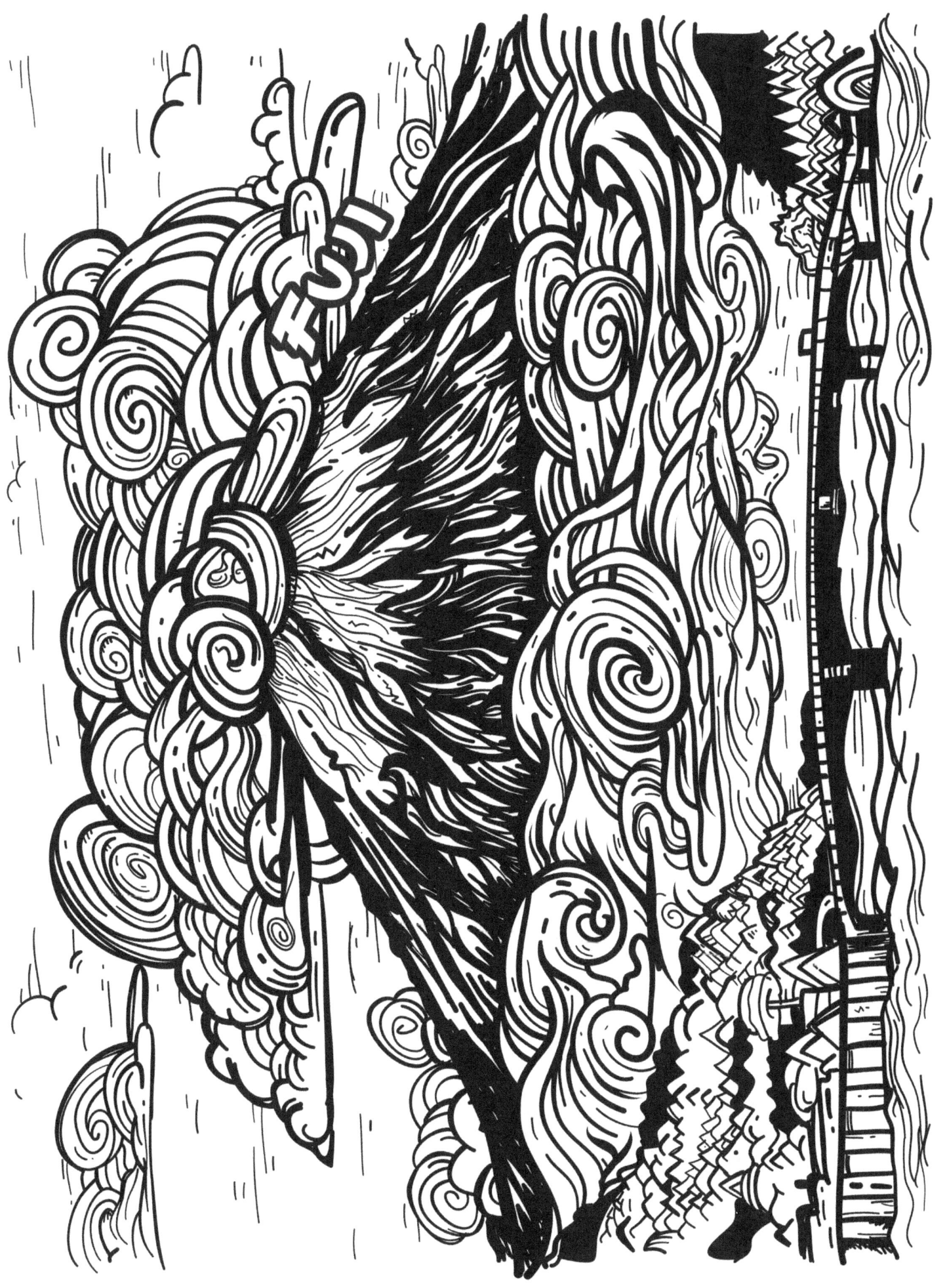

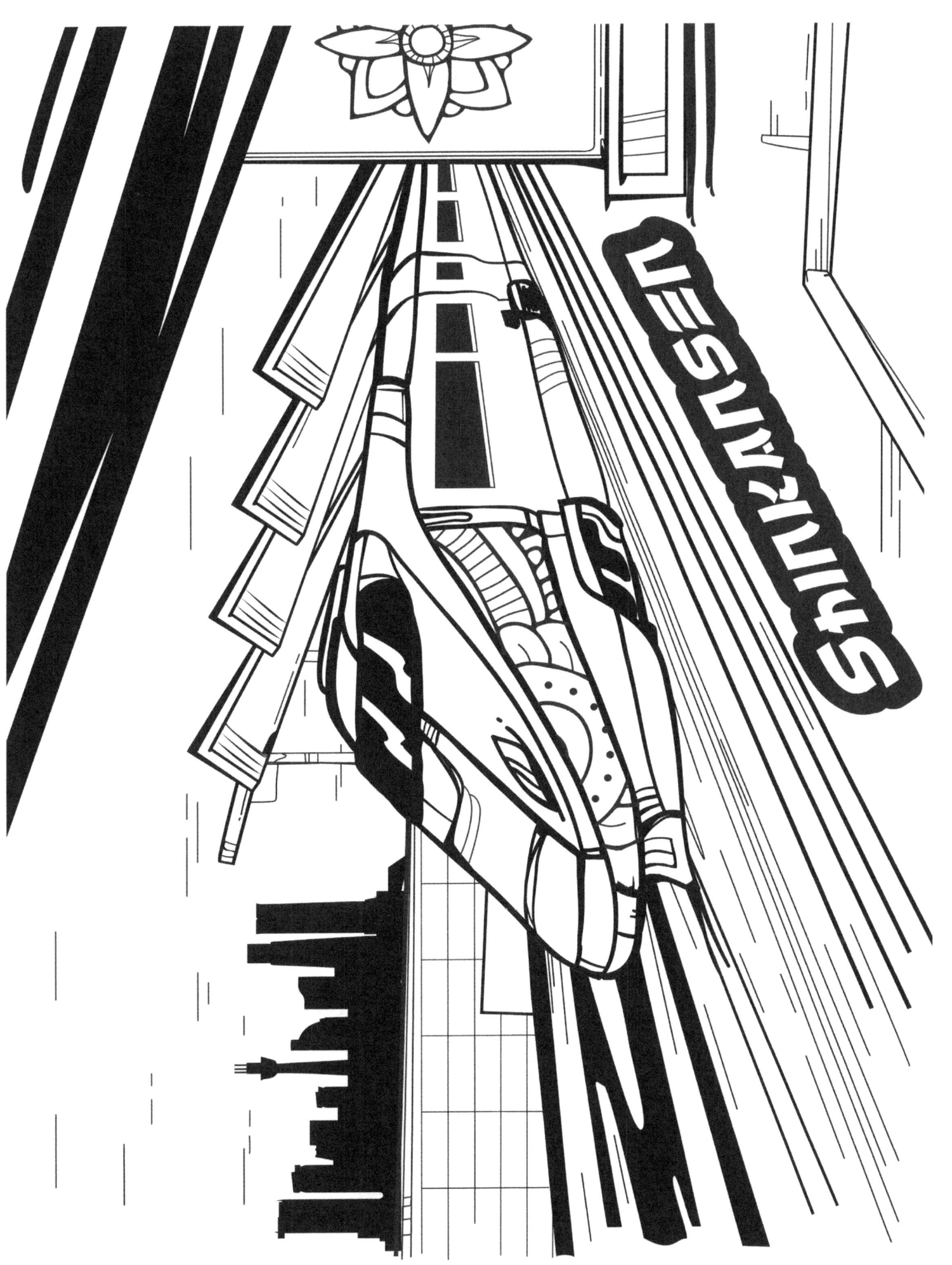

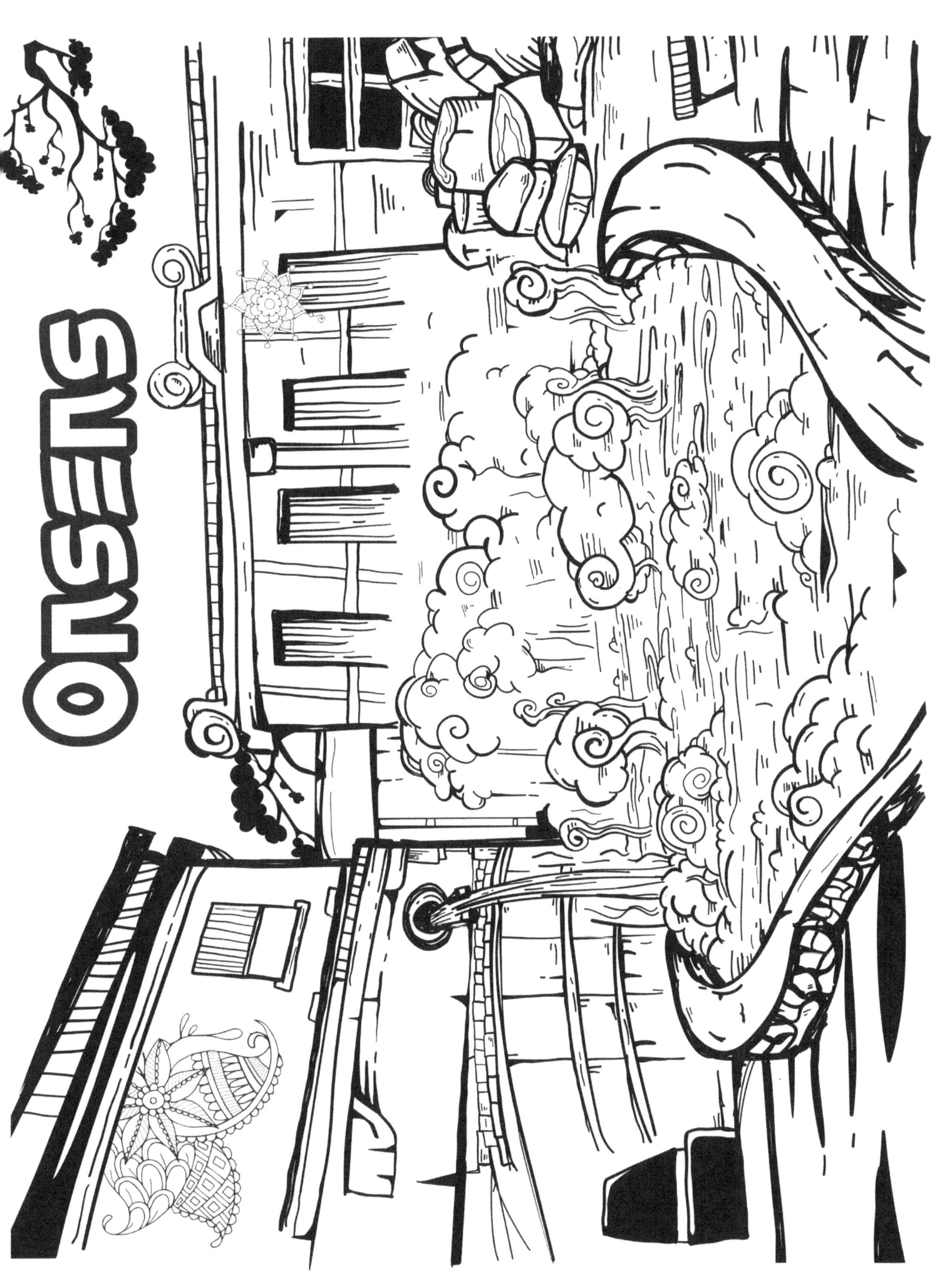

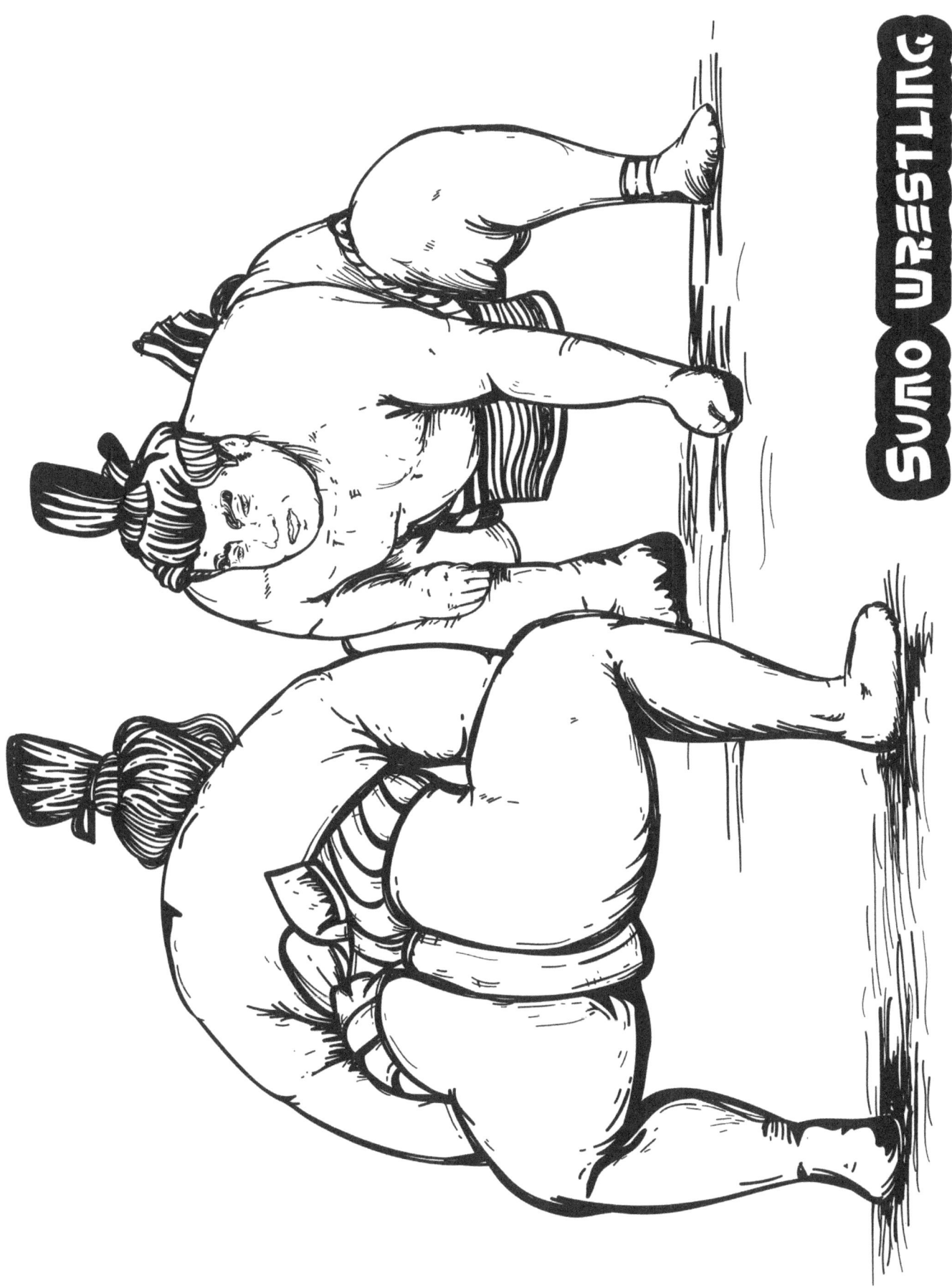

SUMO WRESTLING

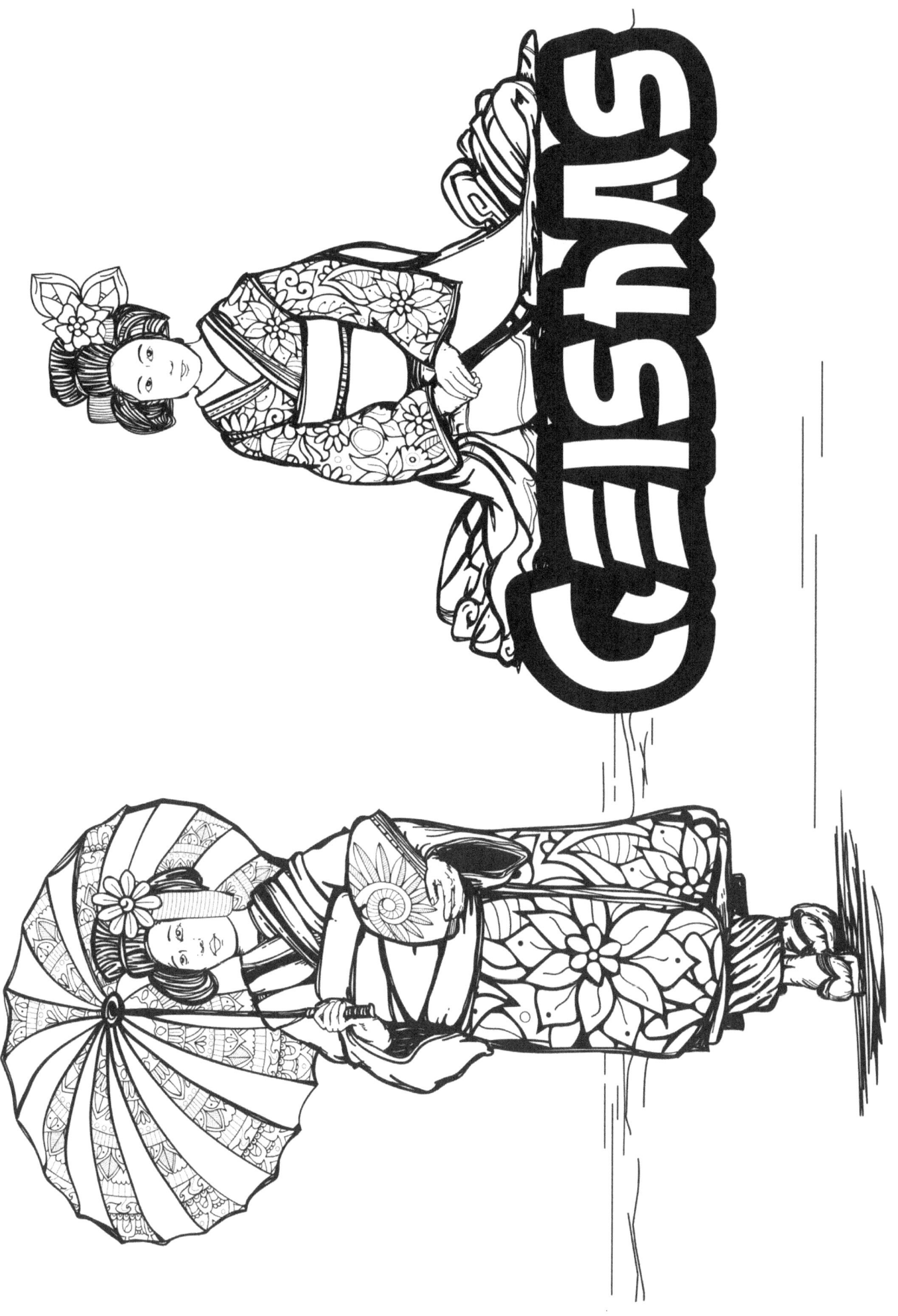

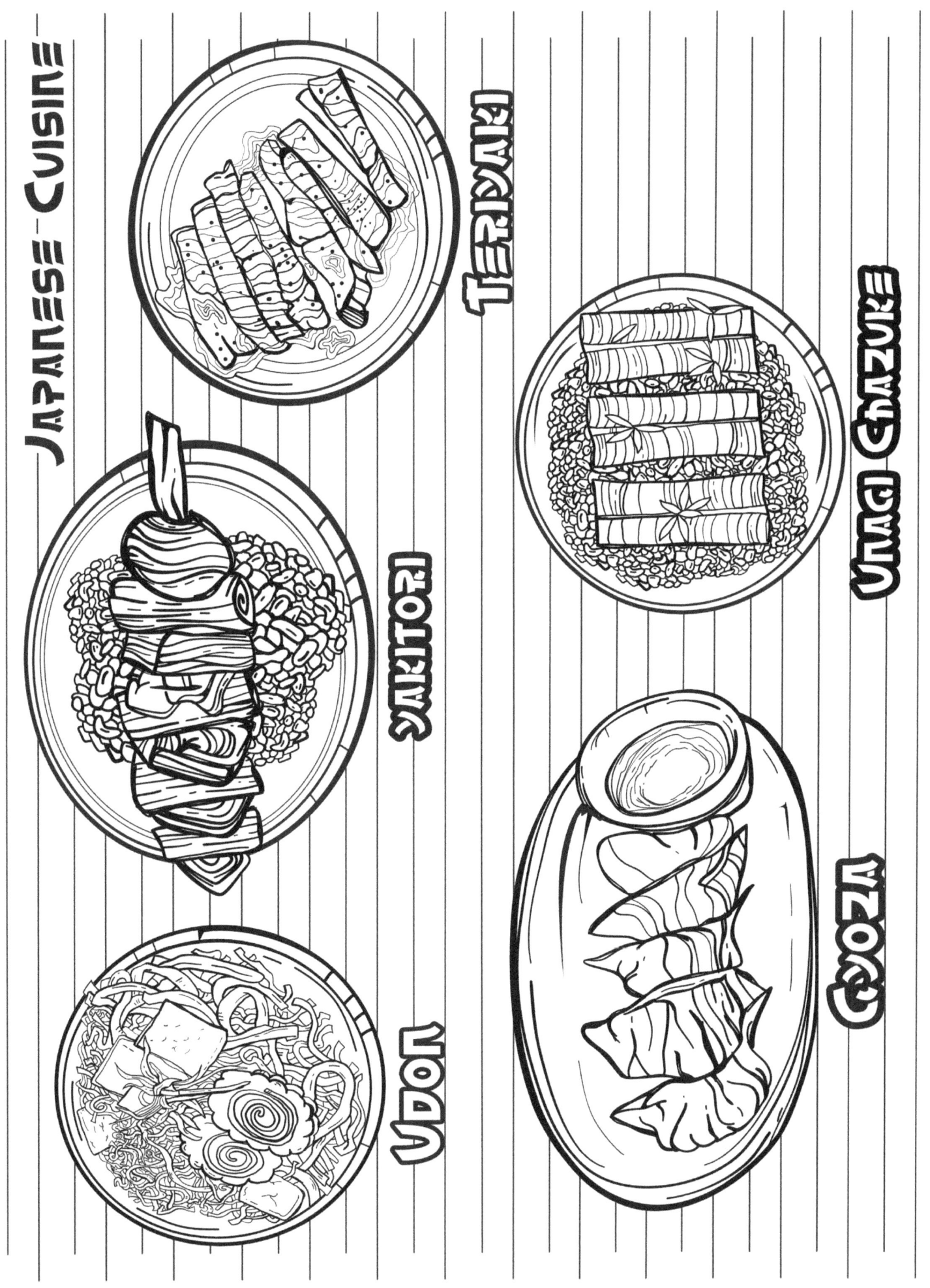

JAPANESE CUISINE

TERIYAKI

UNAGI DONBURI

YAKITORI

GYOZA

UDON

Sushi

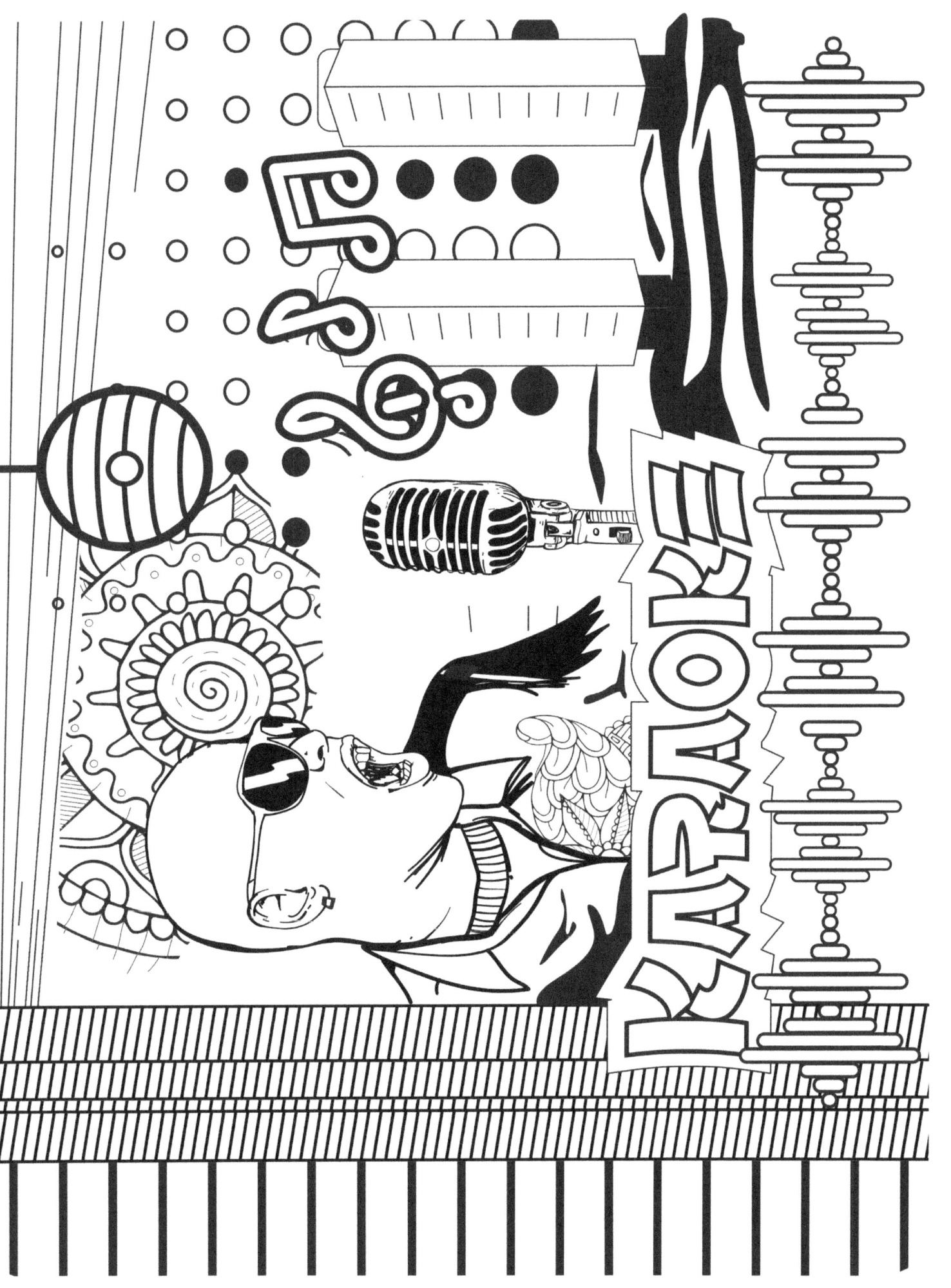

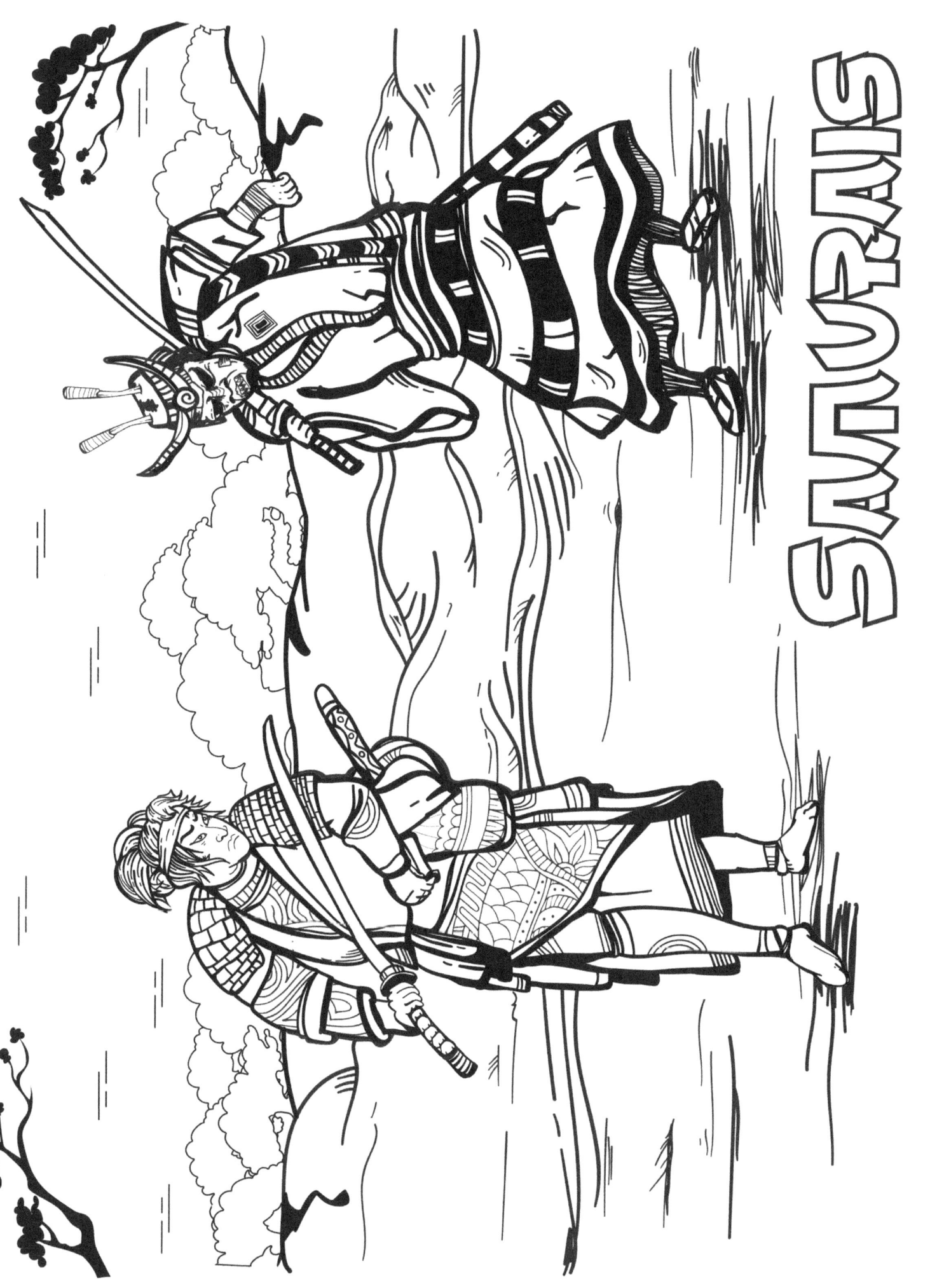

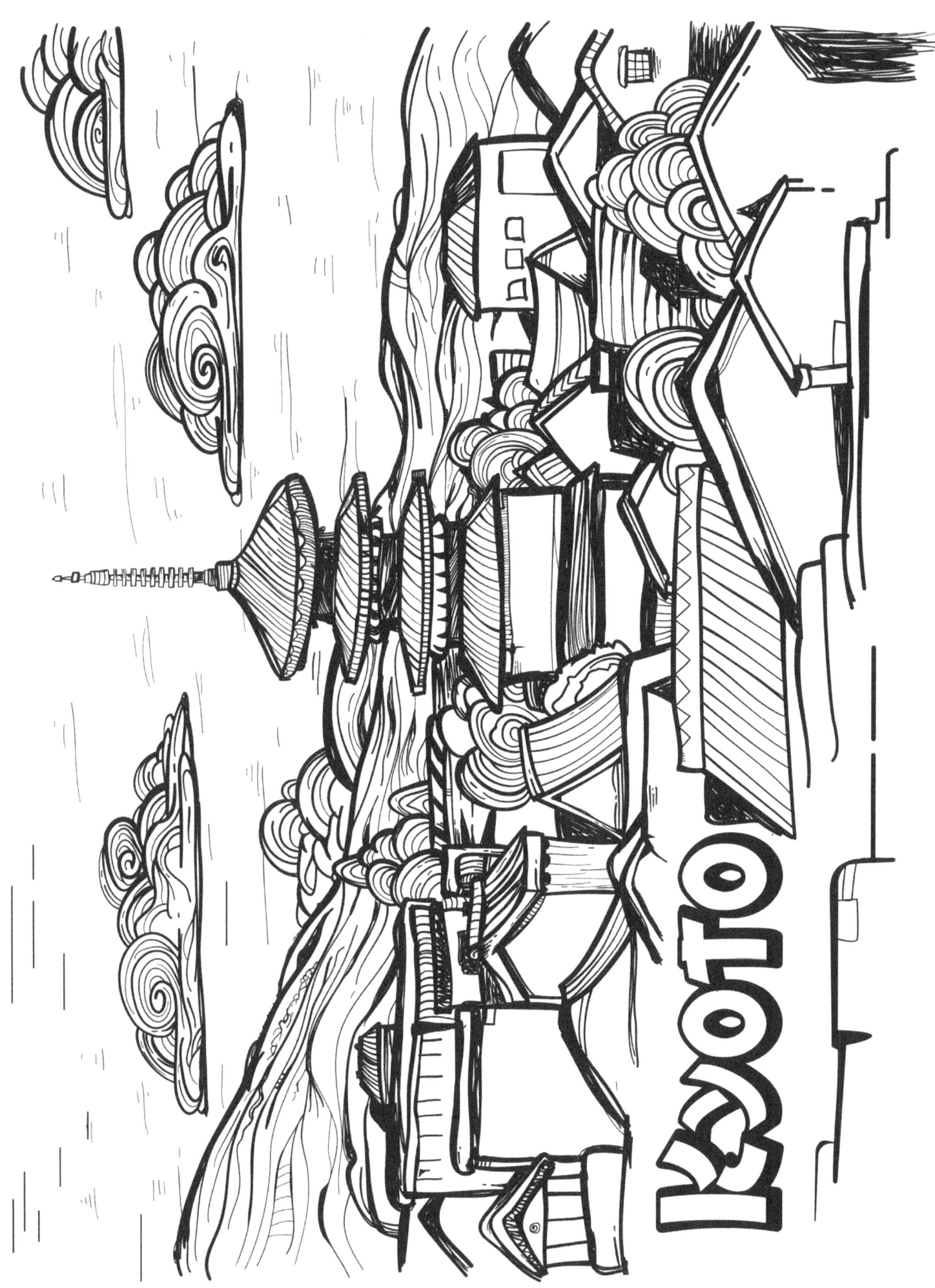

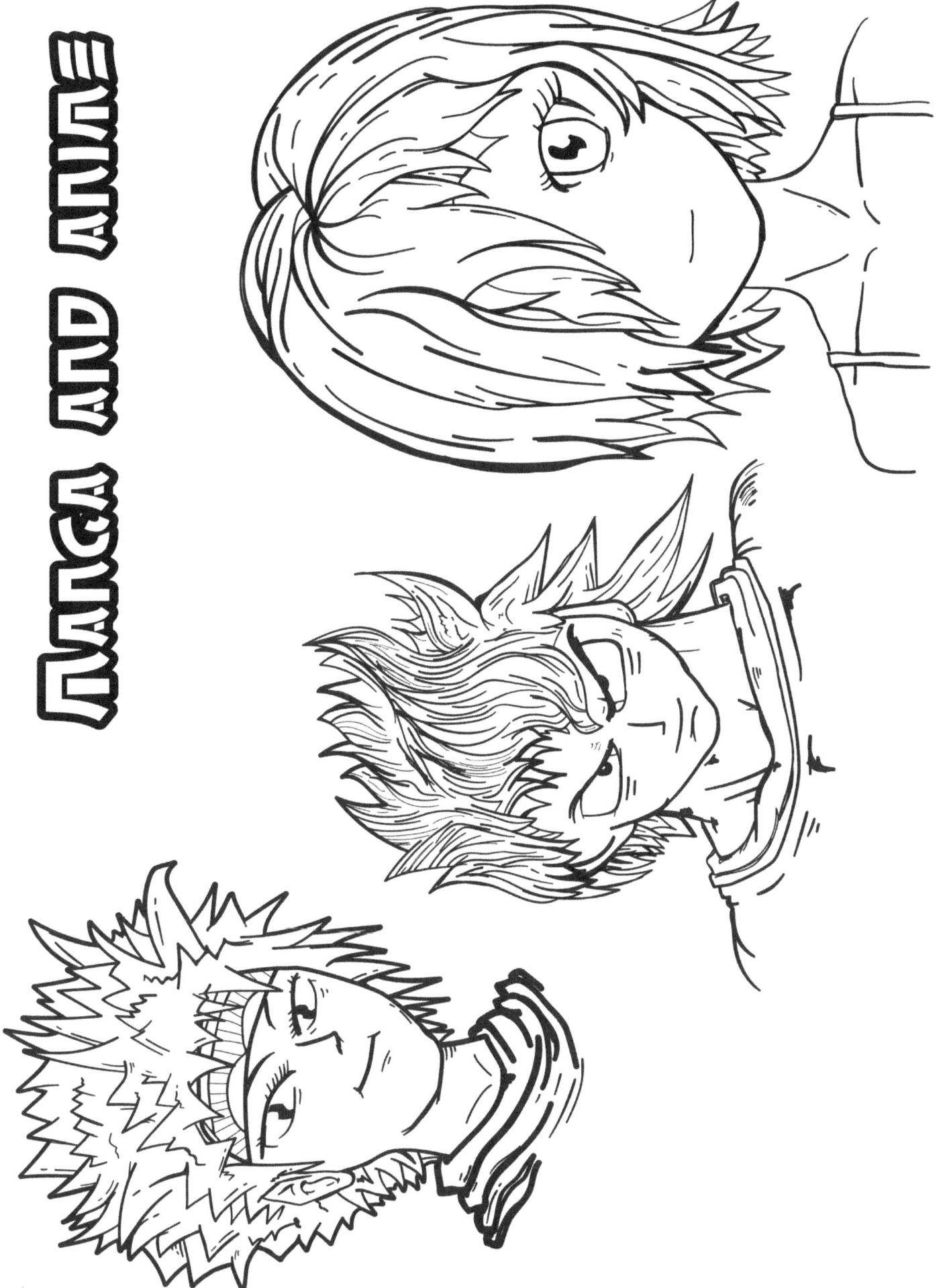

MANGA AND ANIME

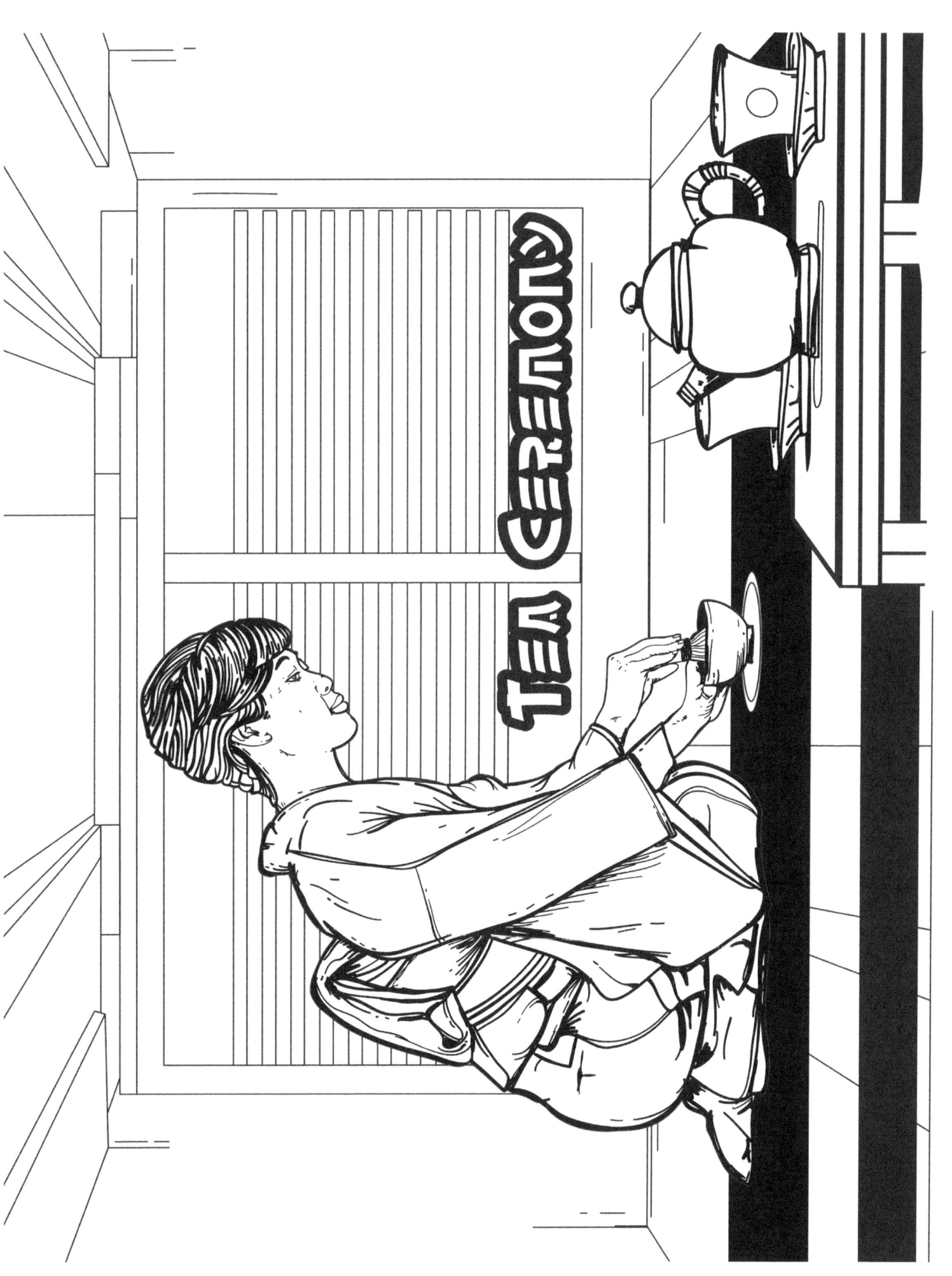

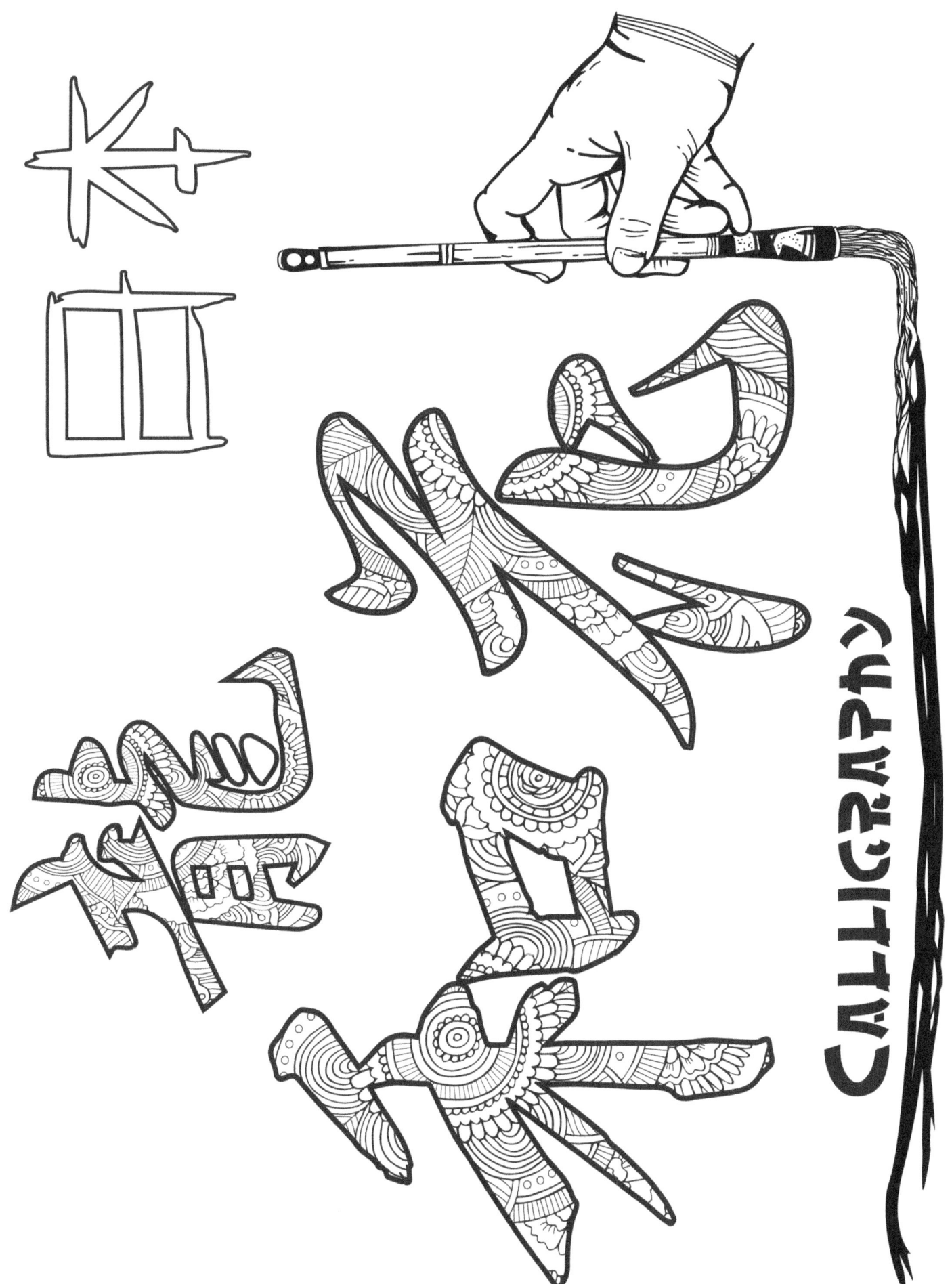

CALLIGRAPHY

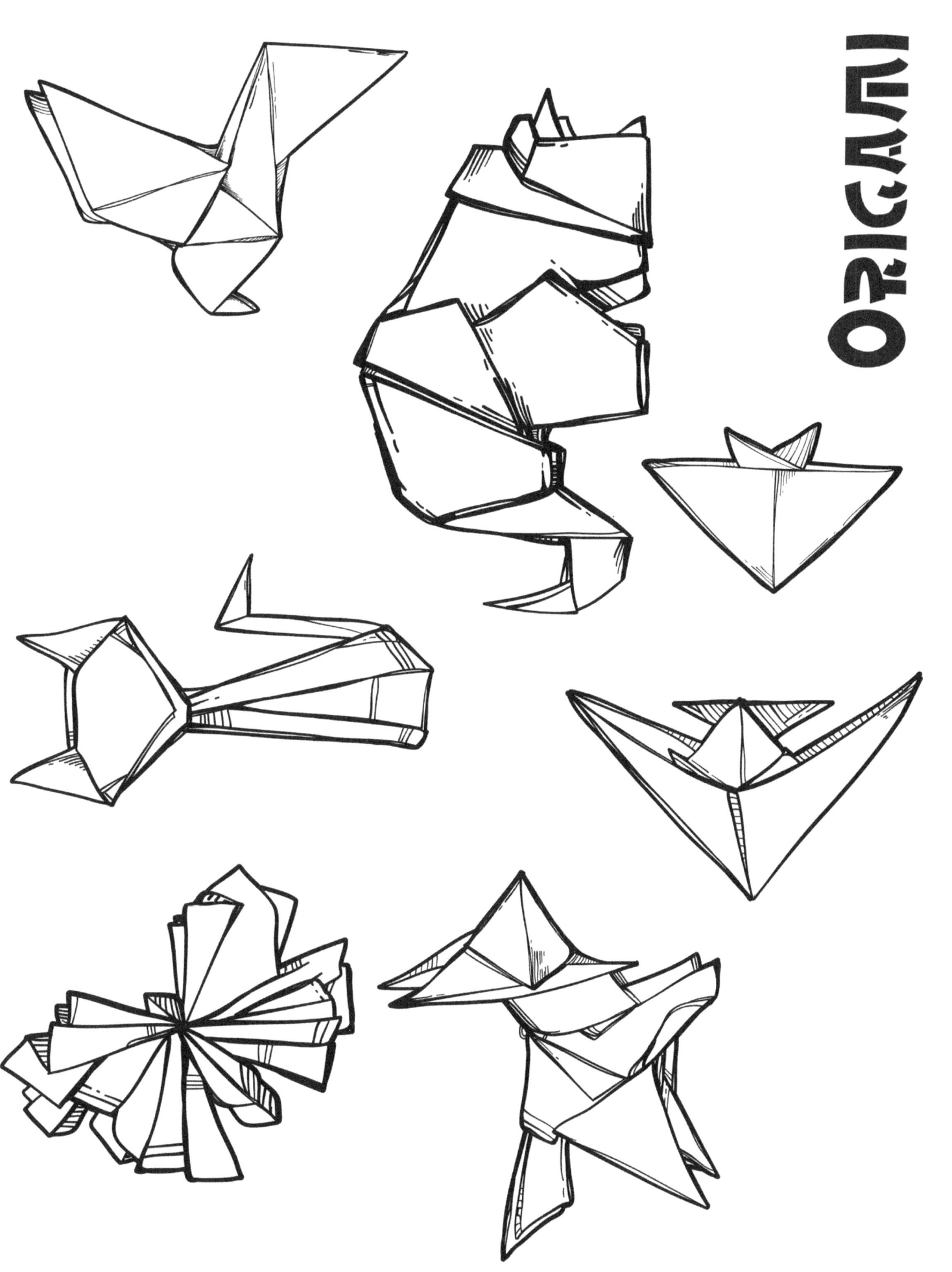

ORIGAMI

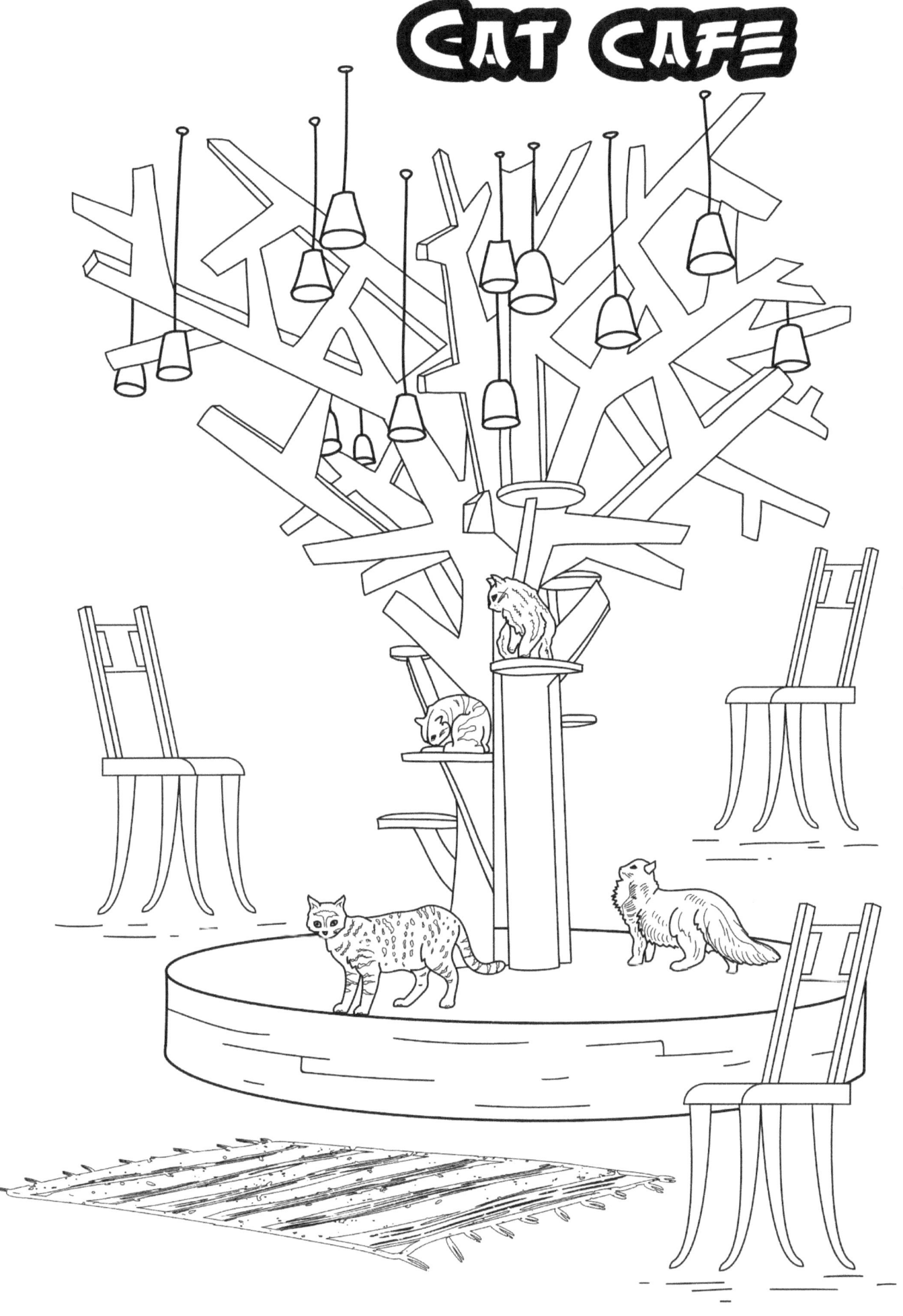

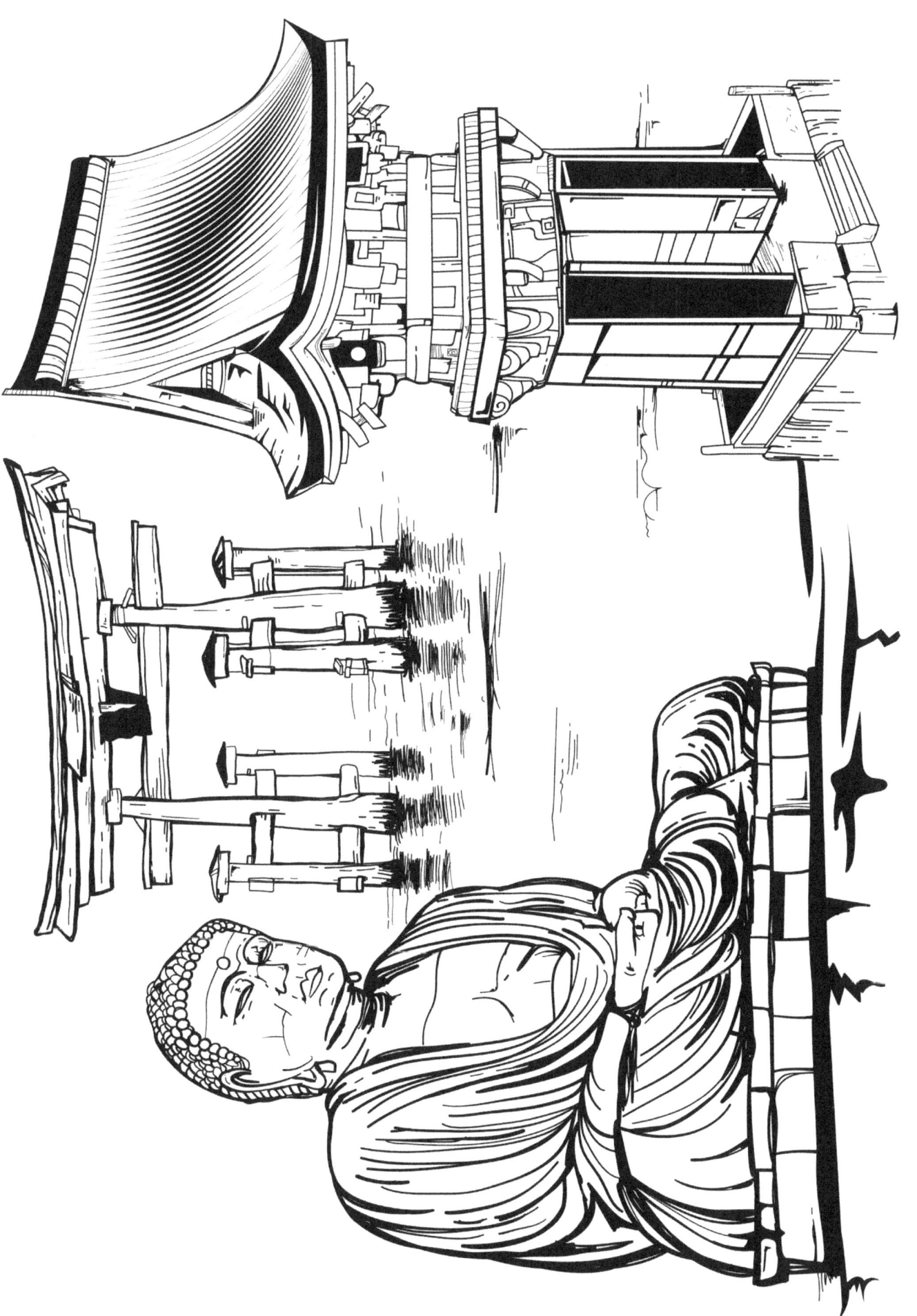

BUDDHIST TEMPLES

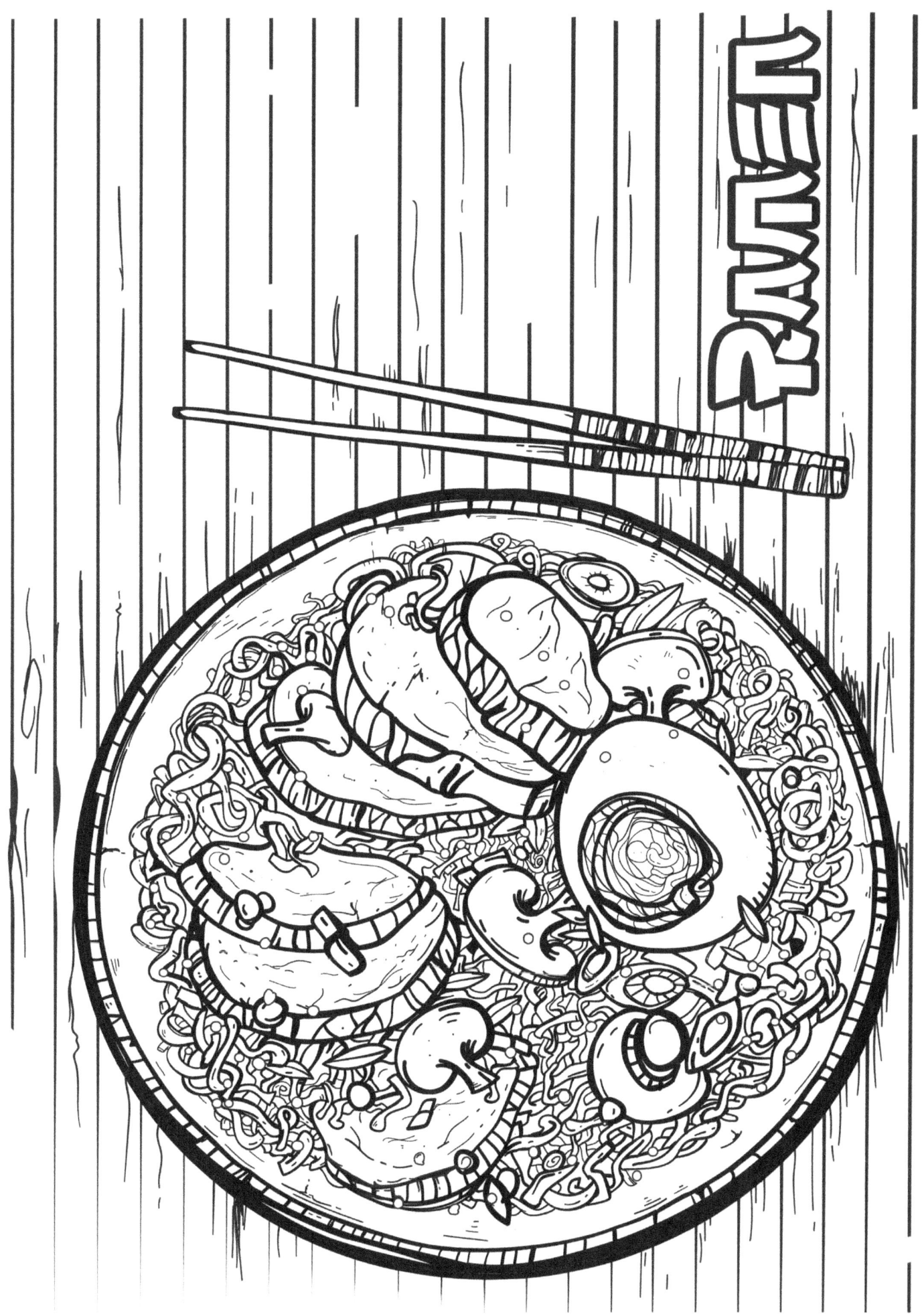

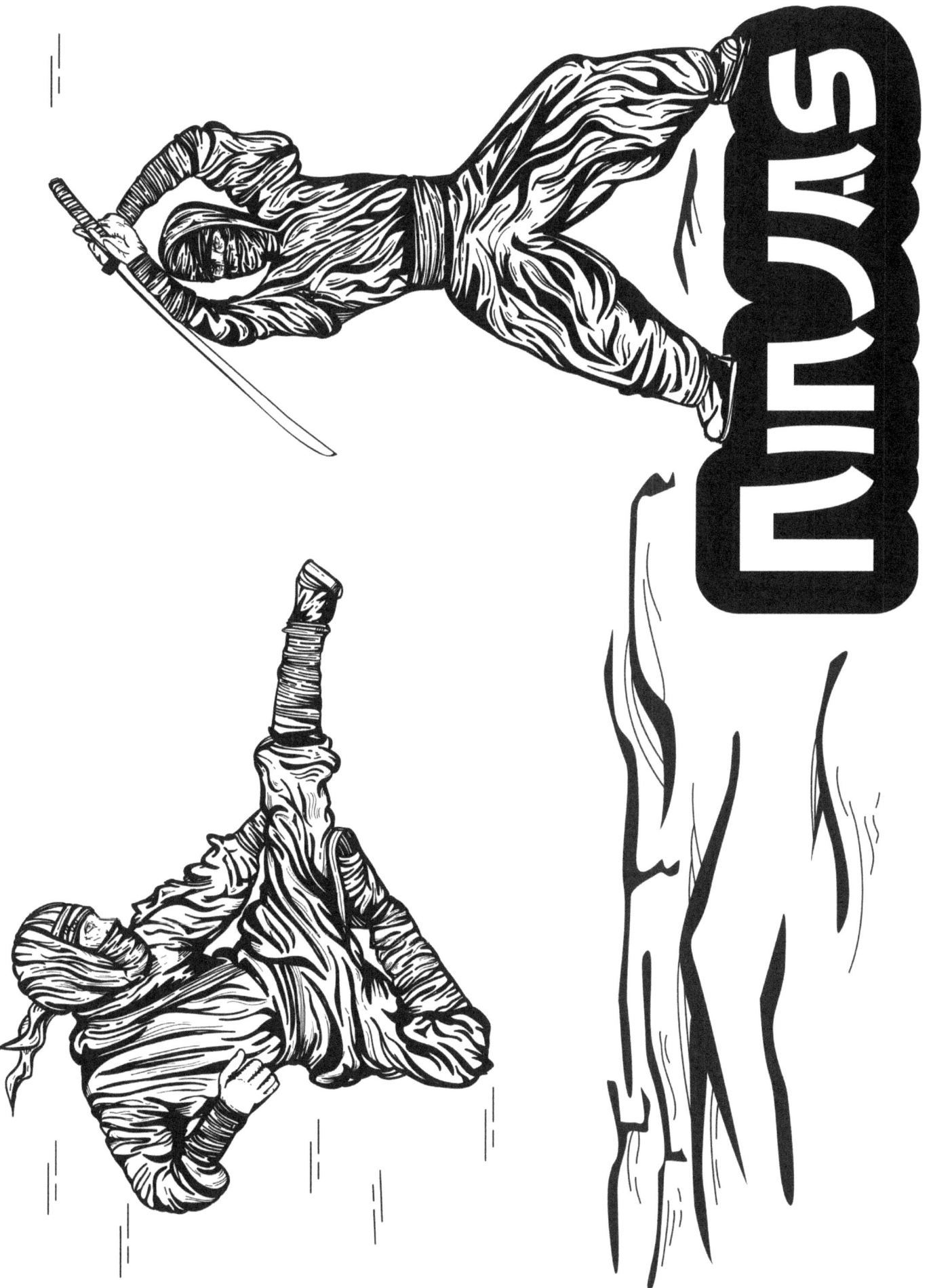

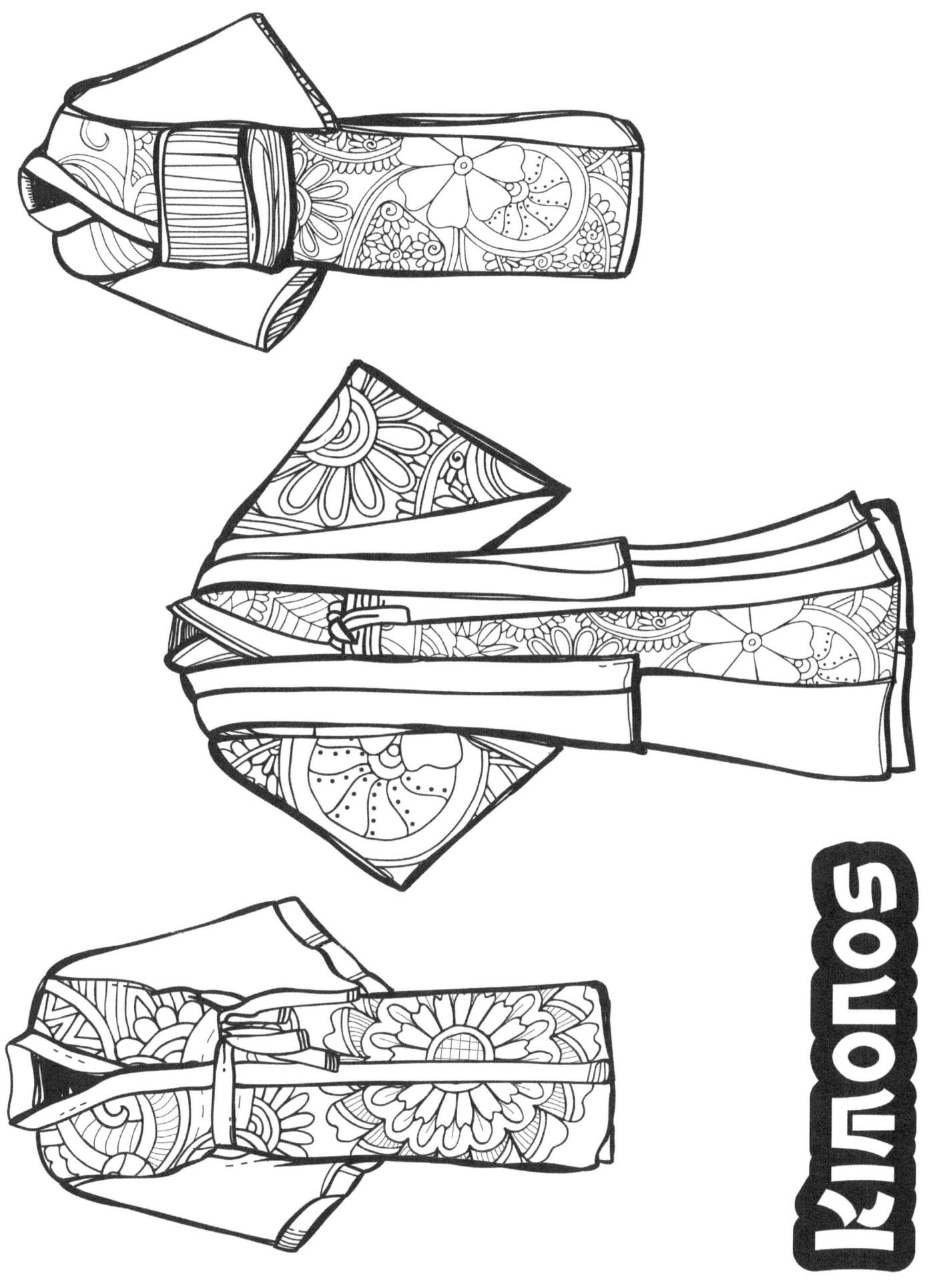

KIMONOS

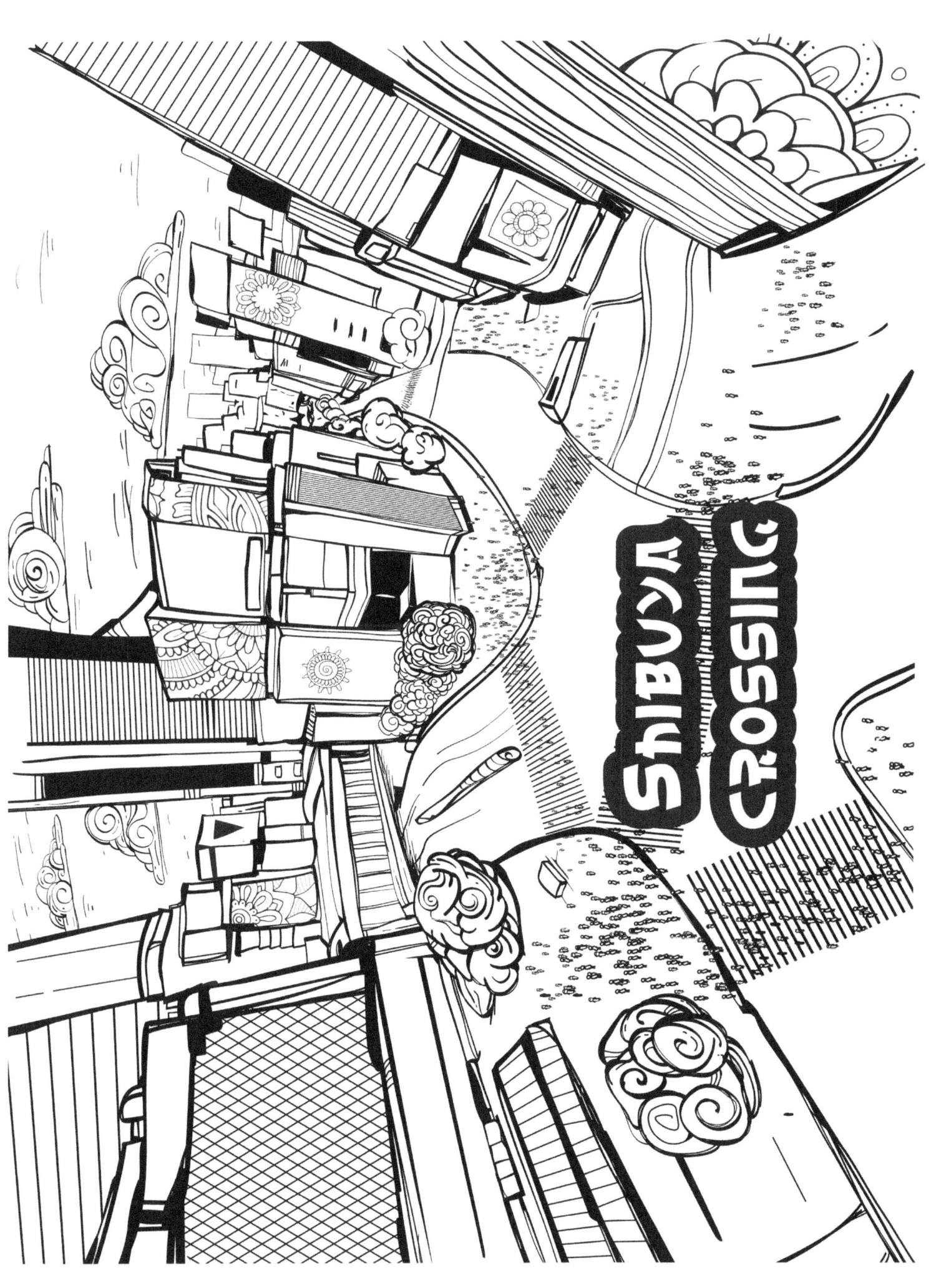

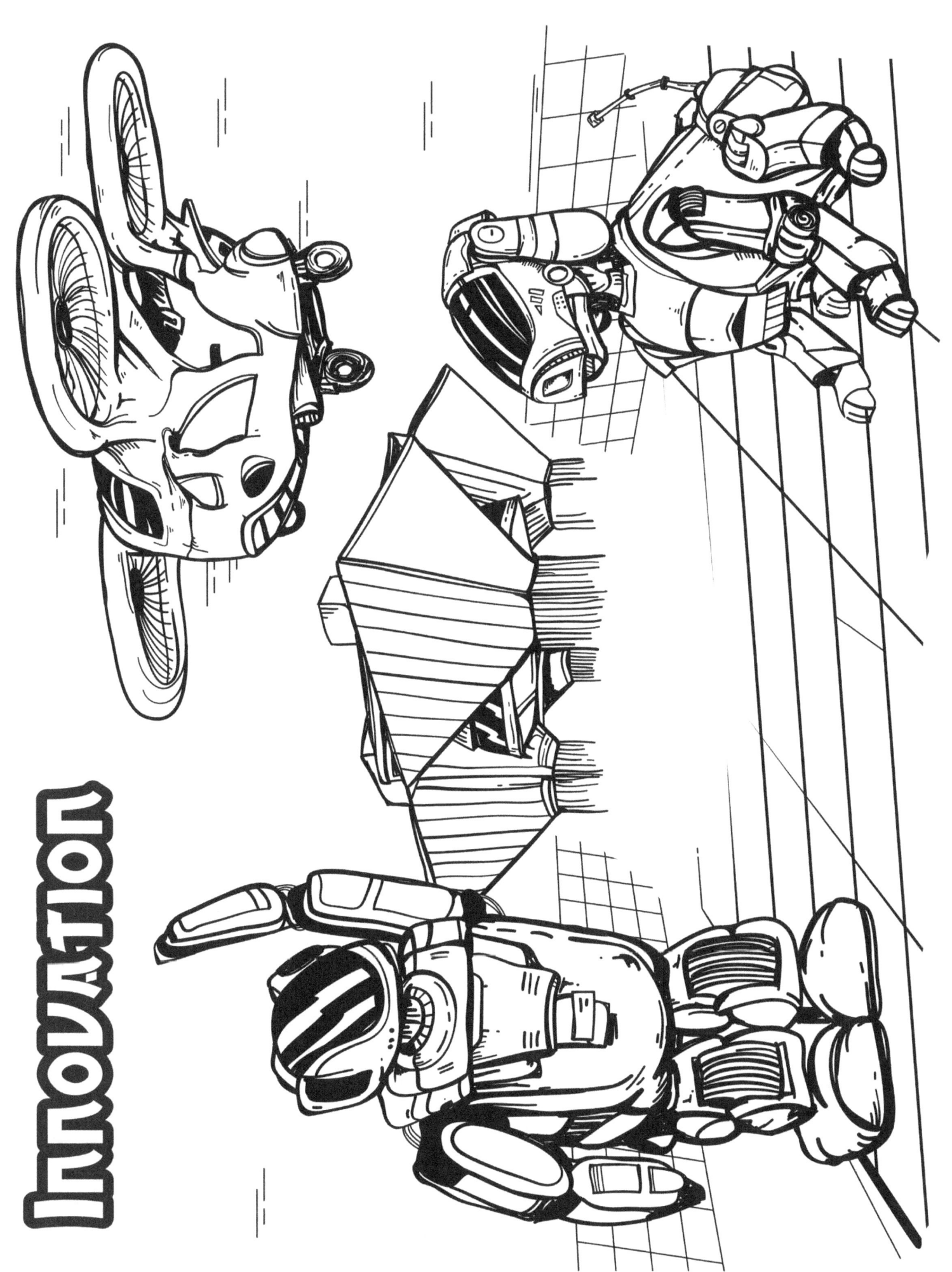

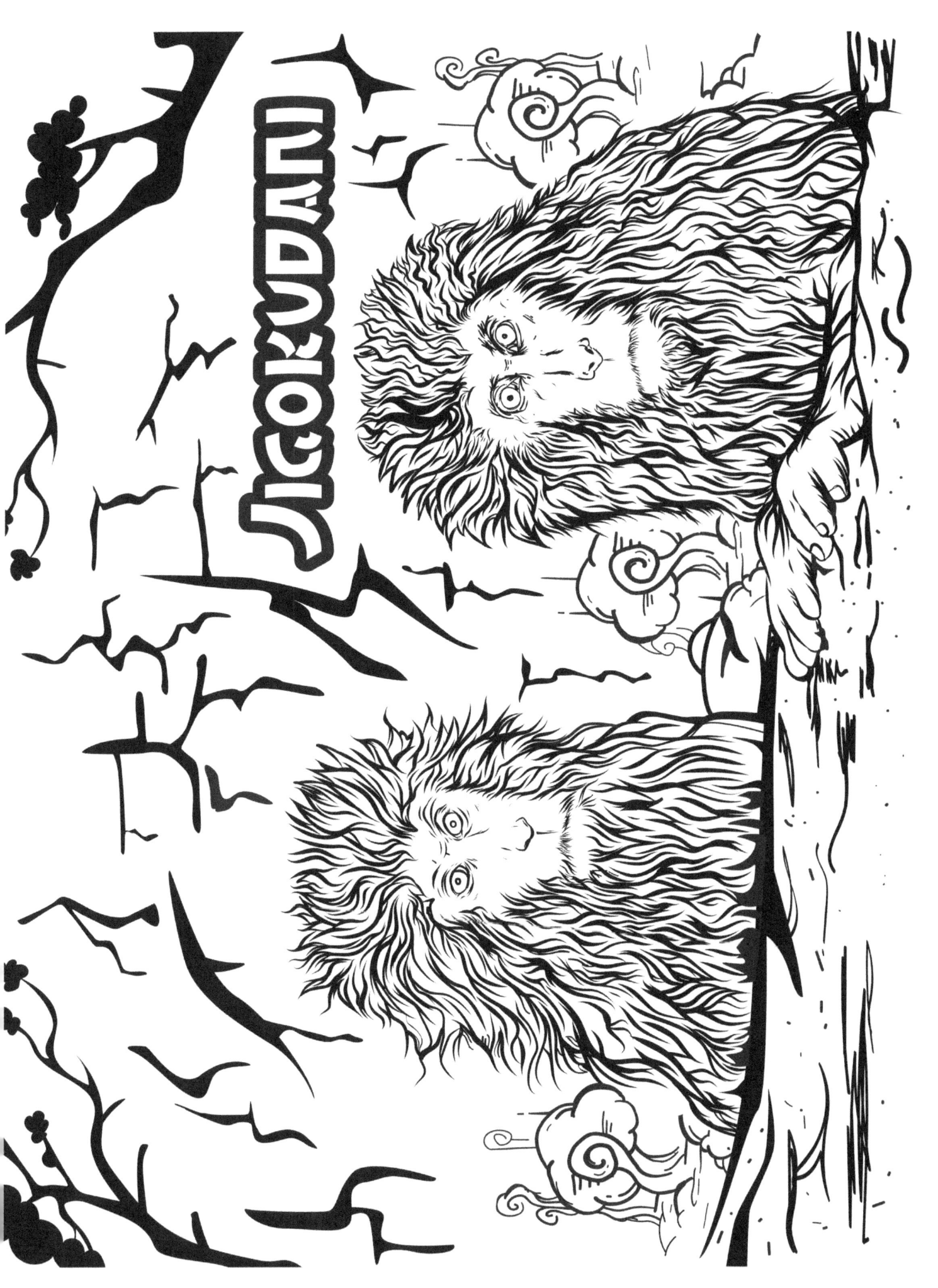

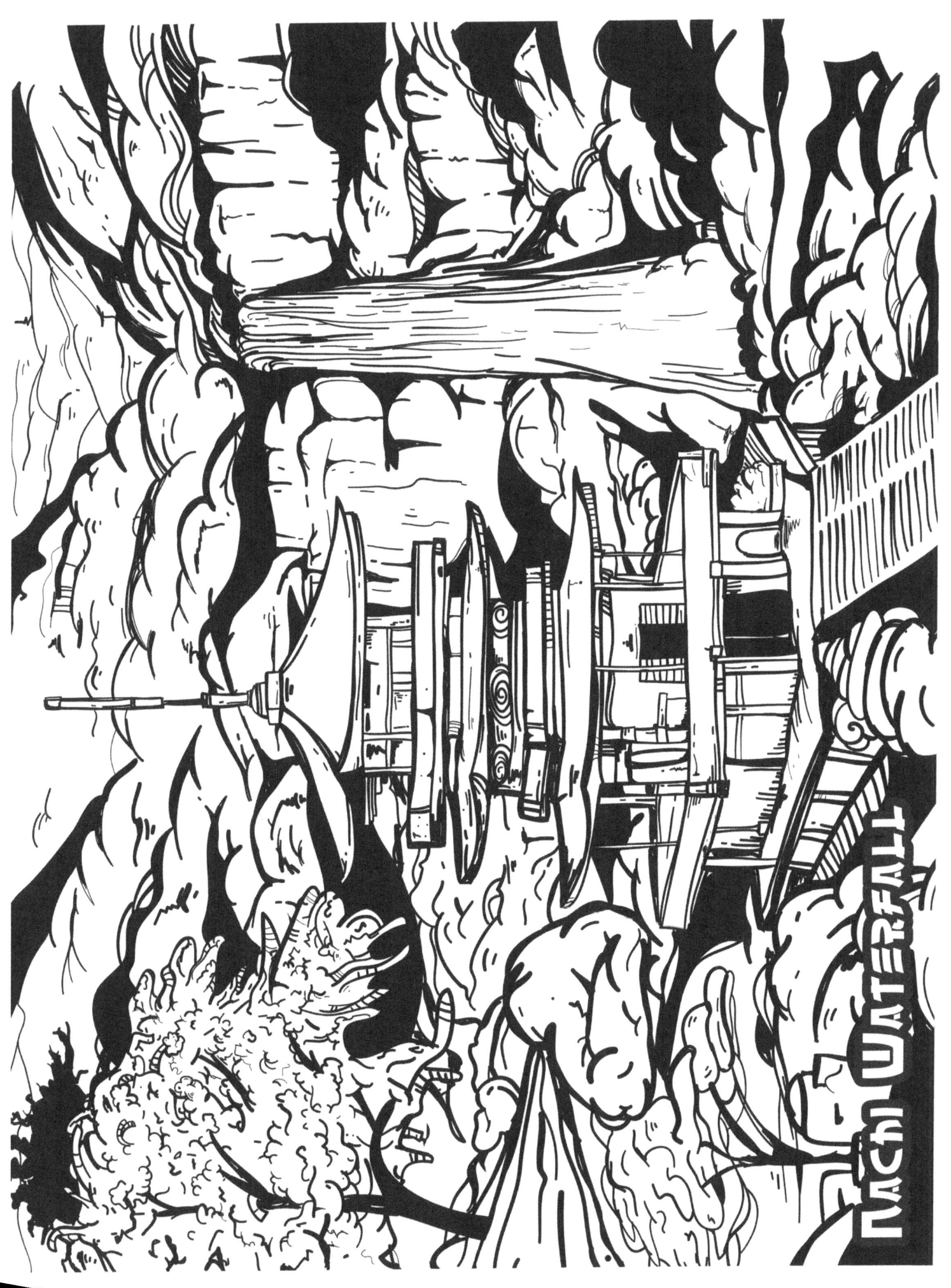

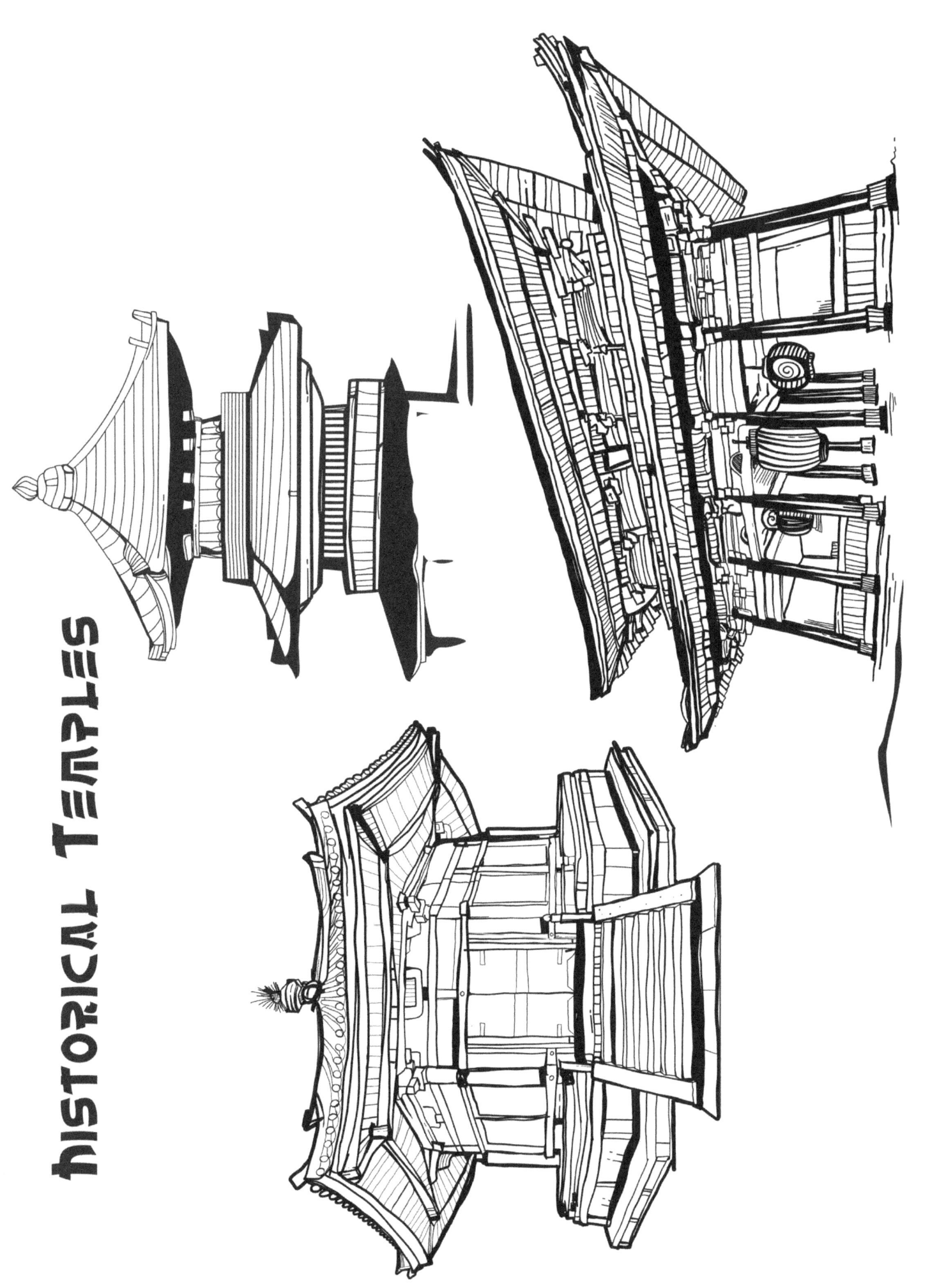

HISTORICAL TEMPLES

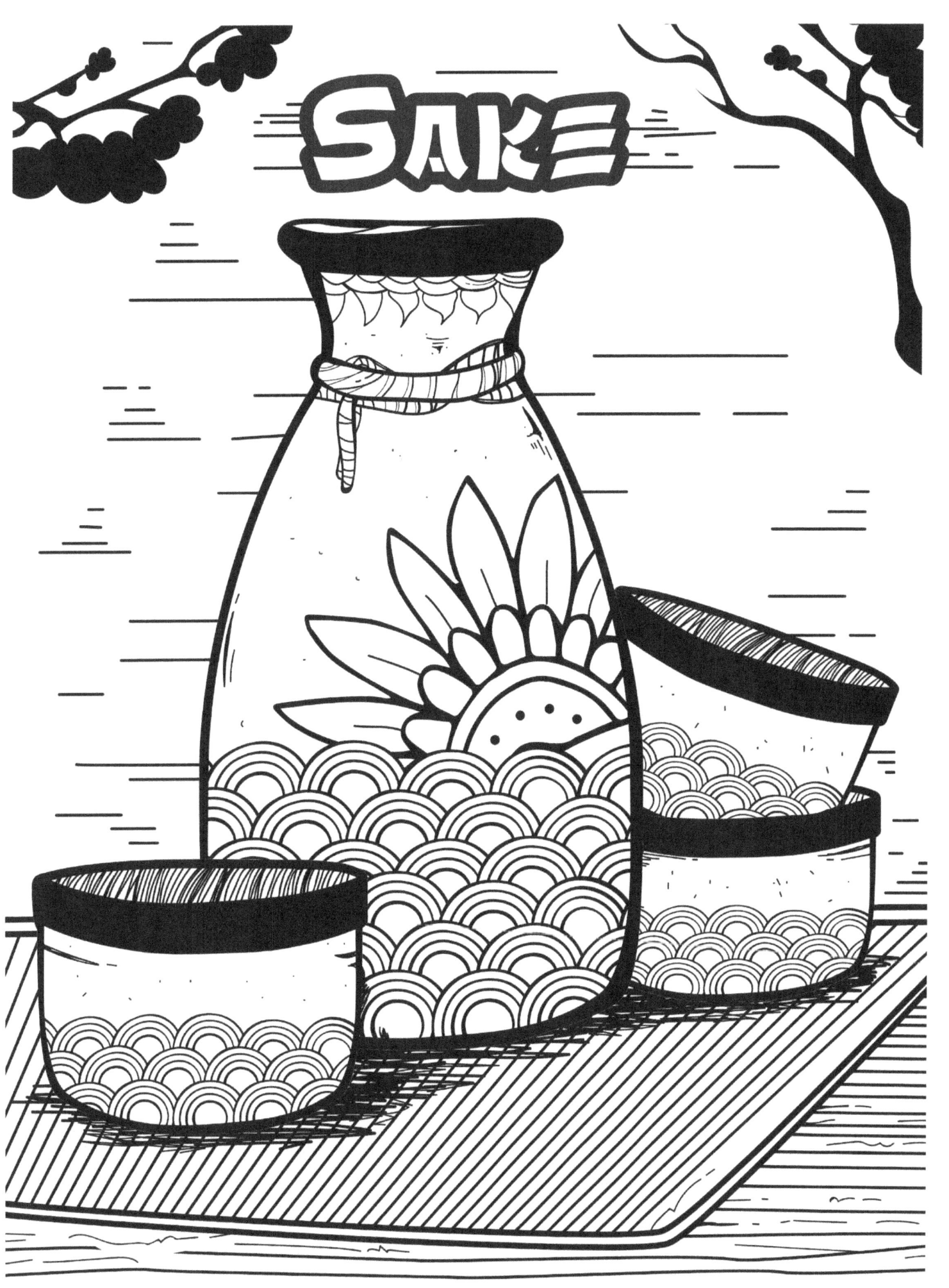

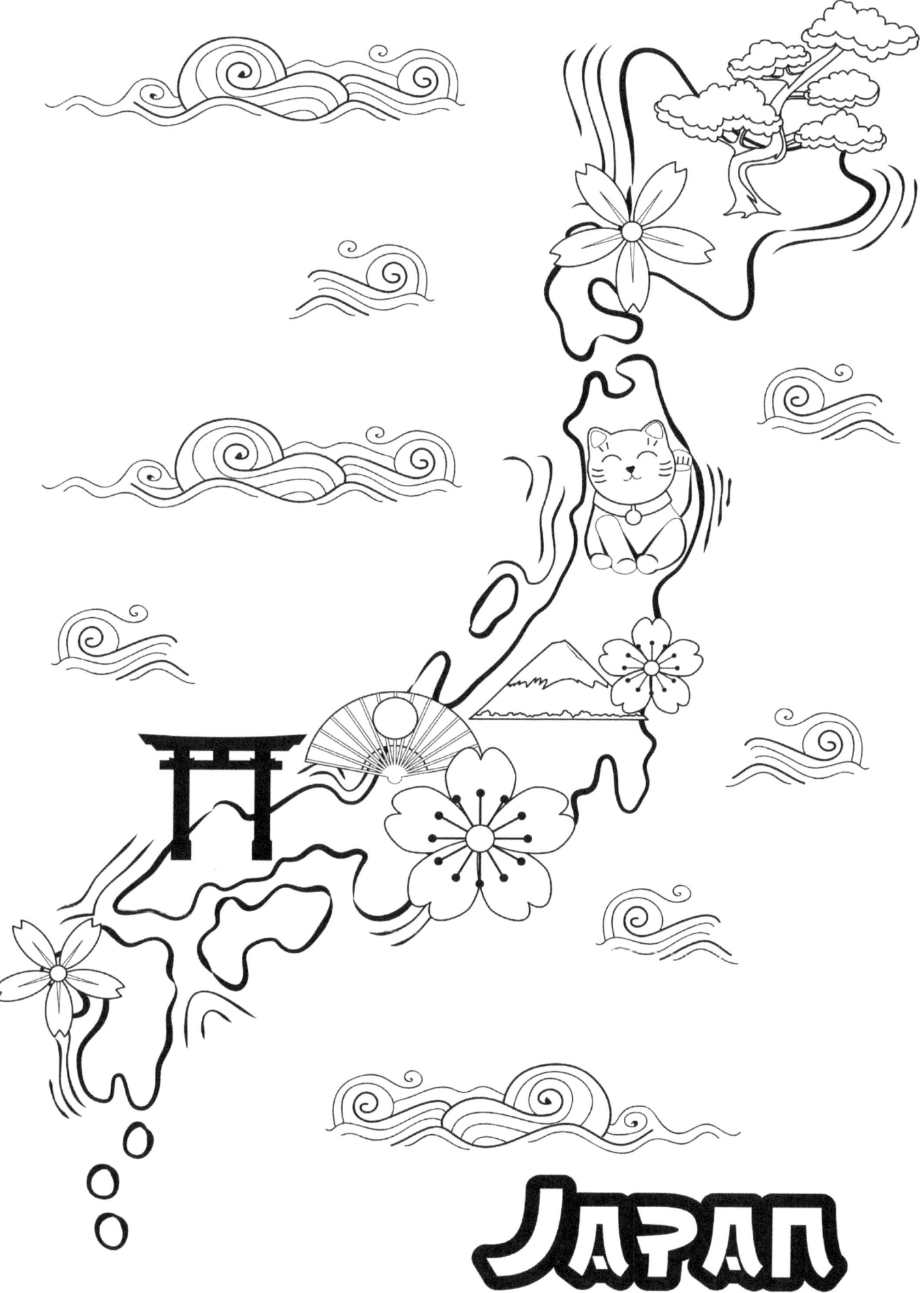

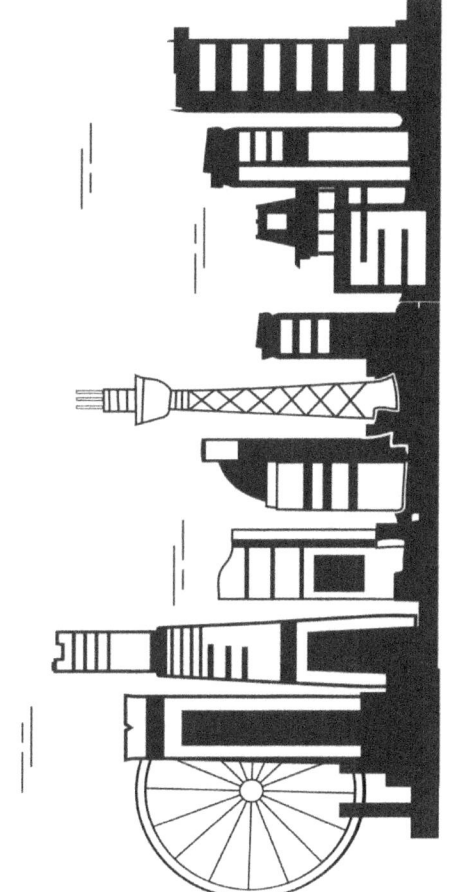

OSAKA

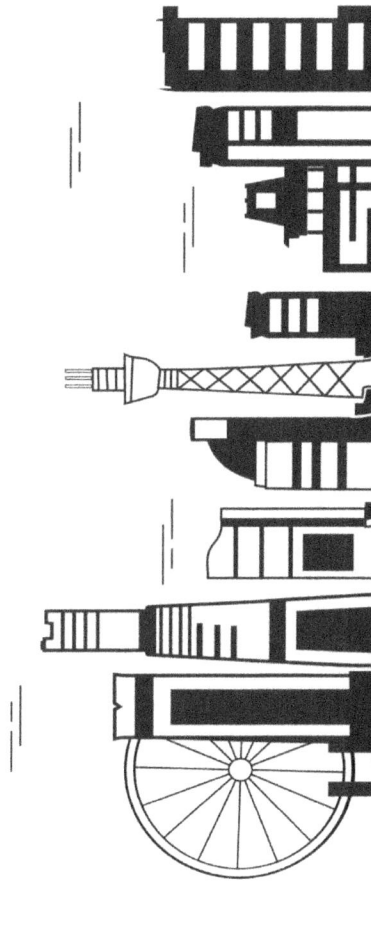

YOKOHAMA

FAMOUS CITIES

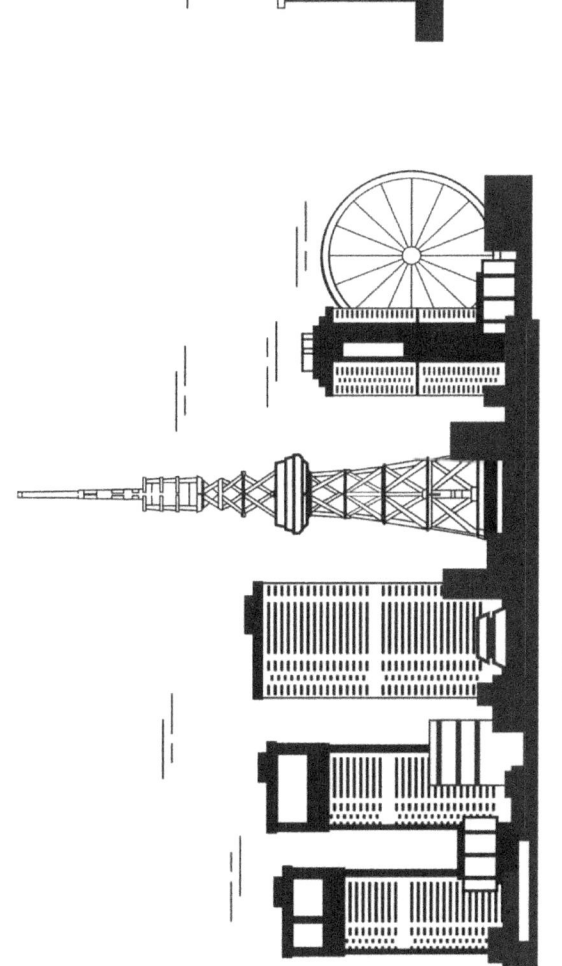

NAGOYA

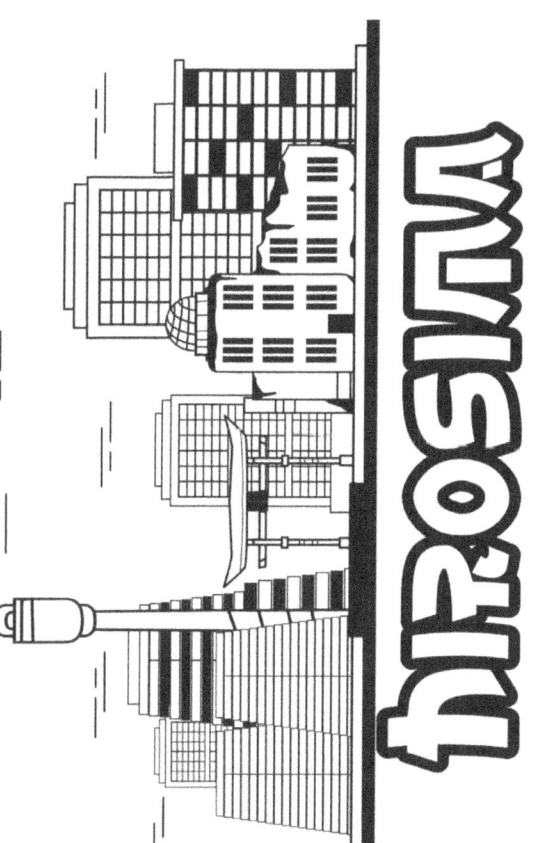

HIROSIMA

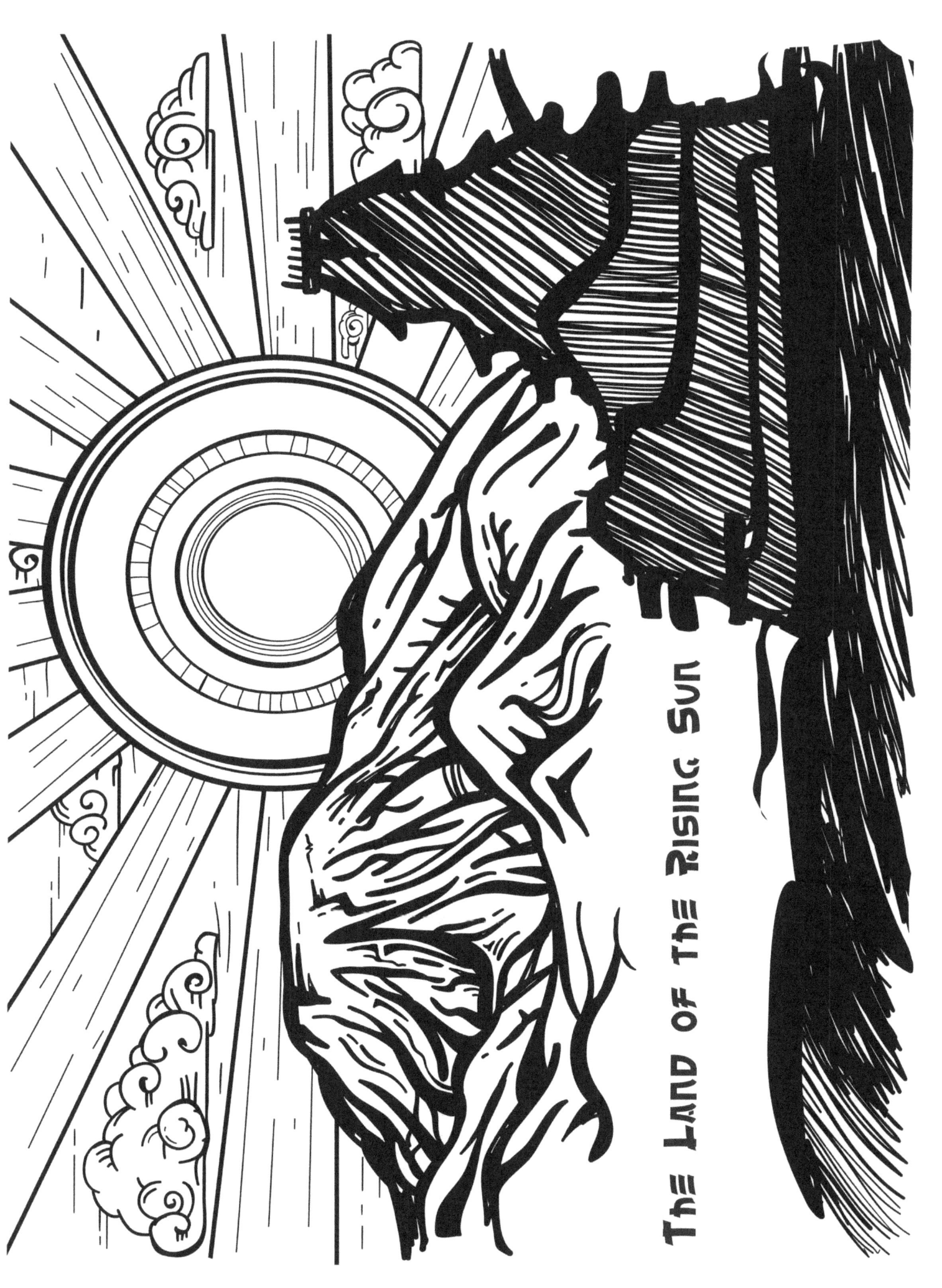

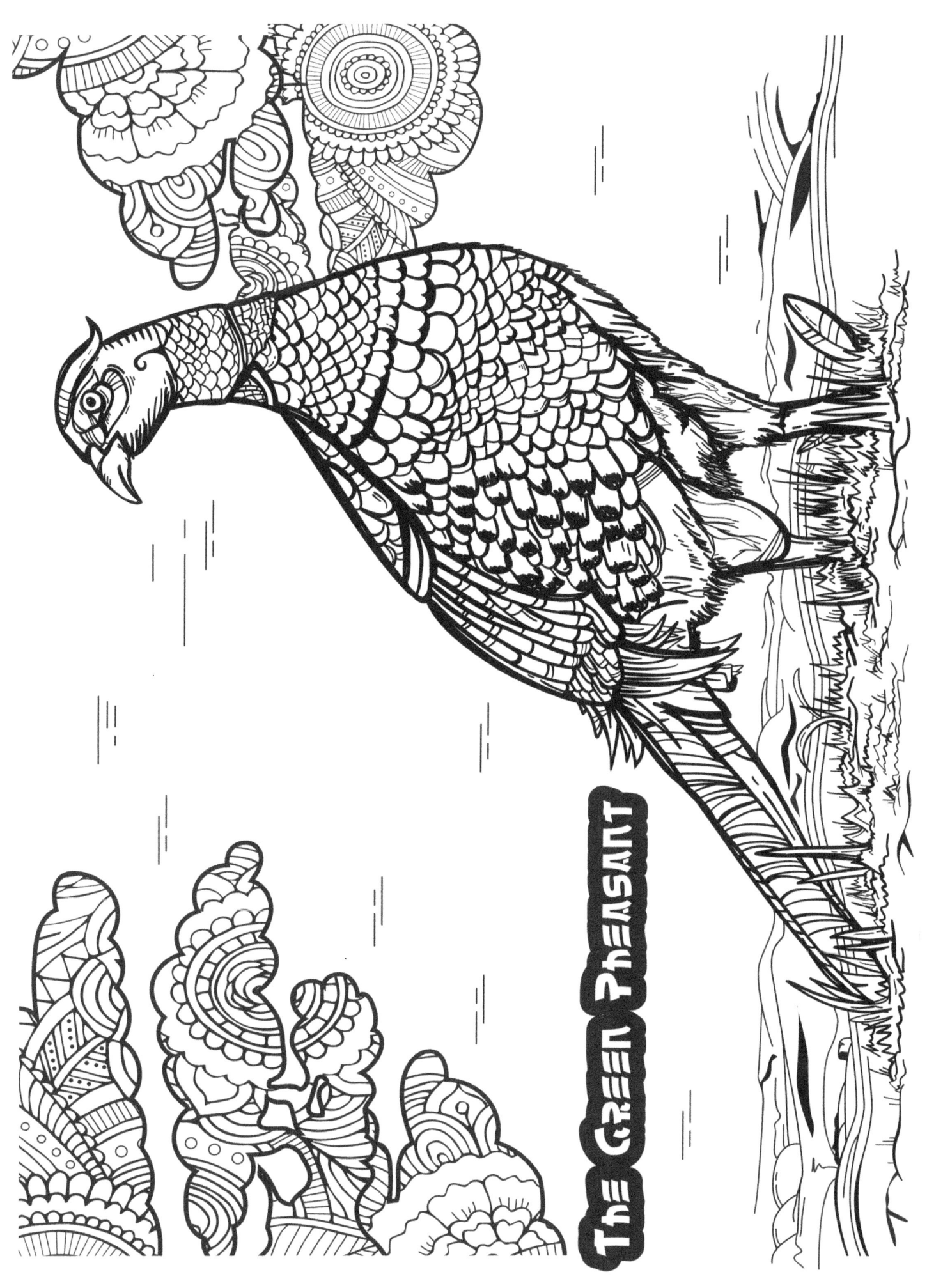

The Green Pheasant

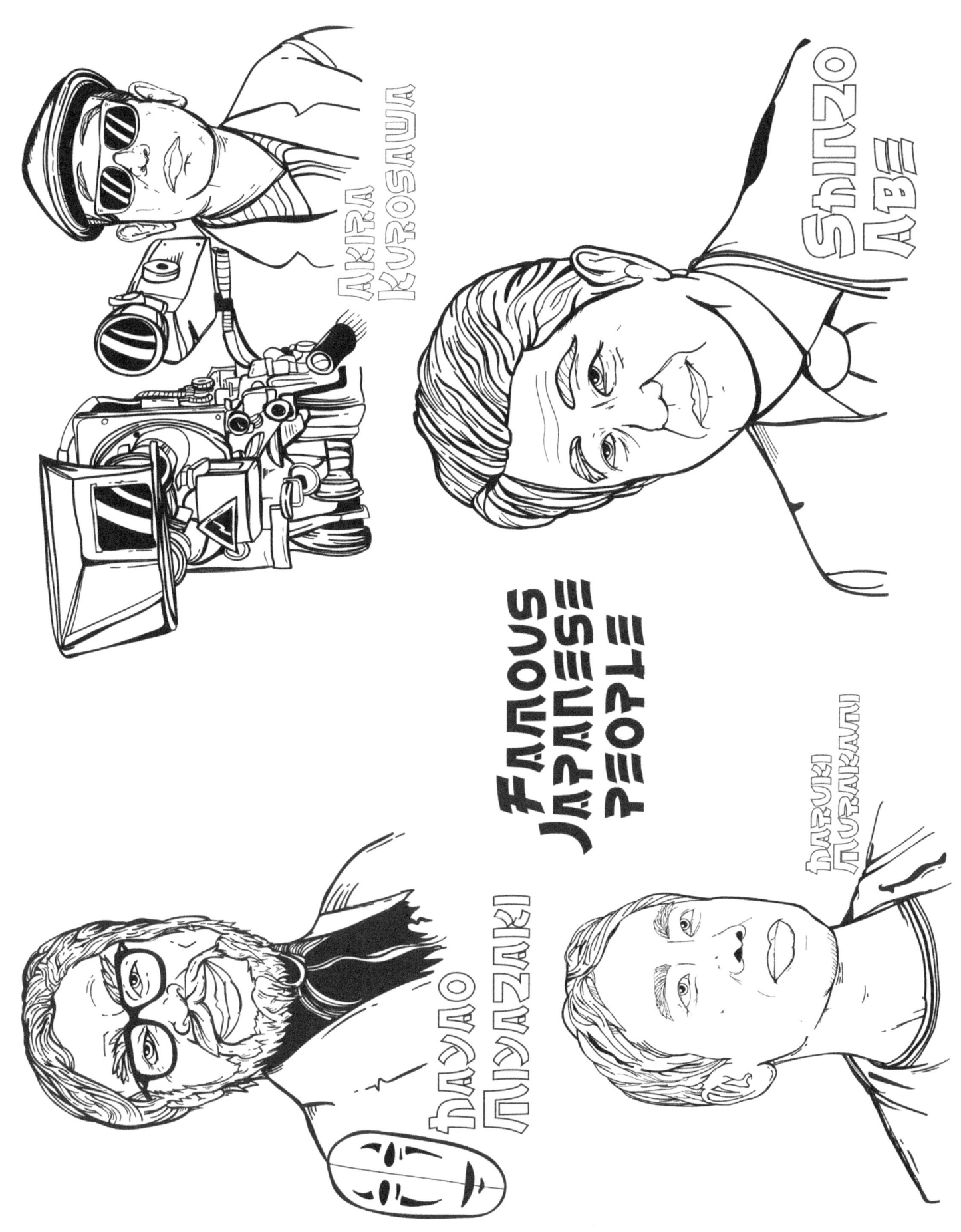

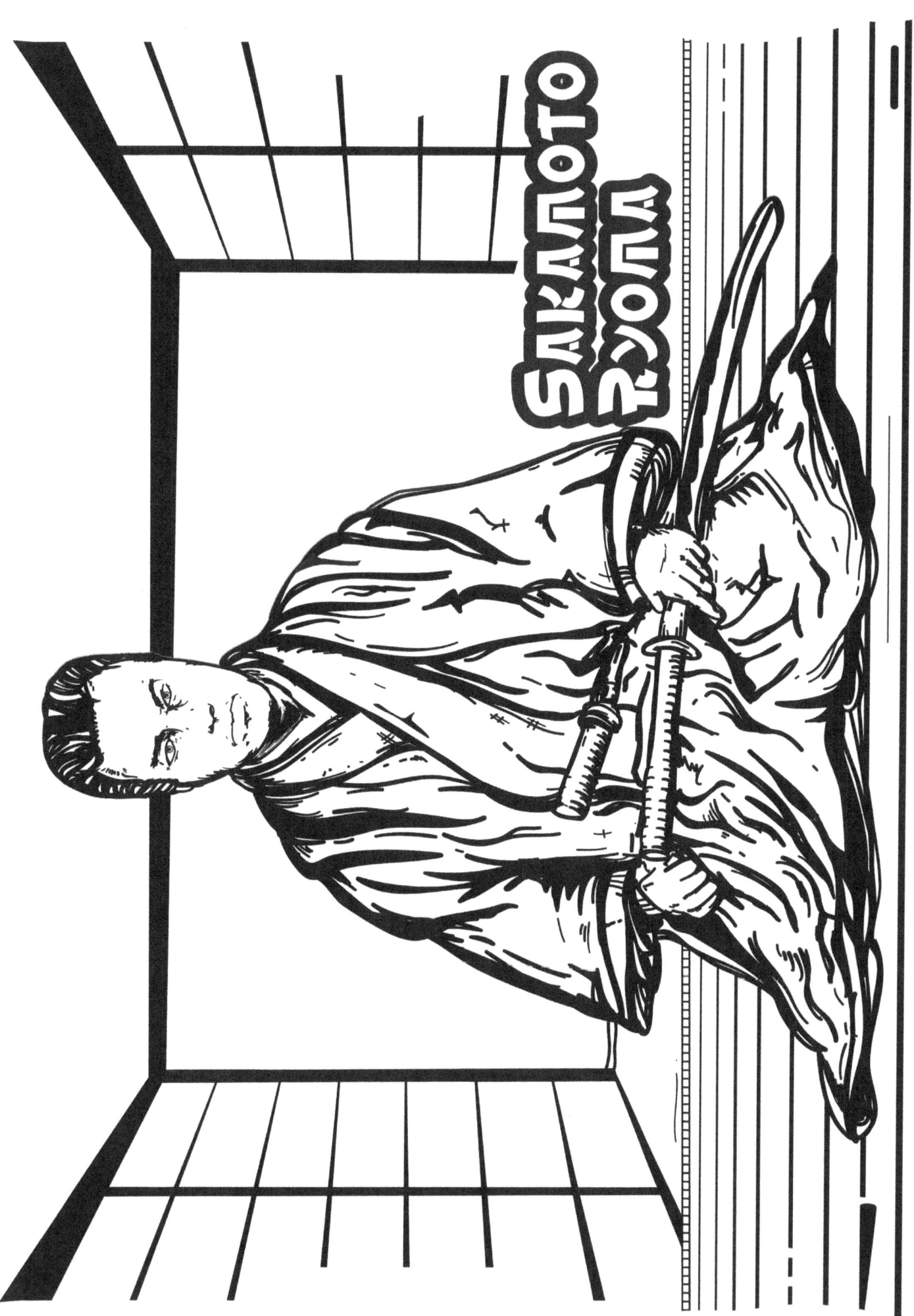

The Maneki-Neko

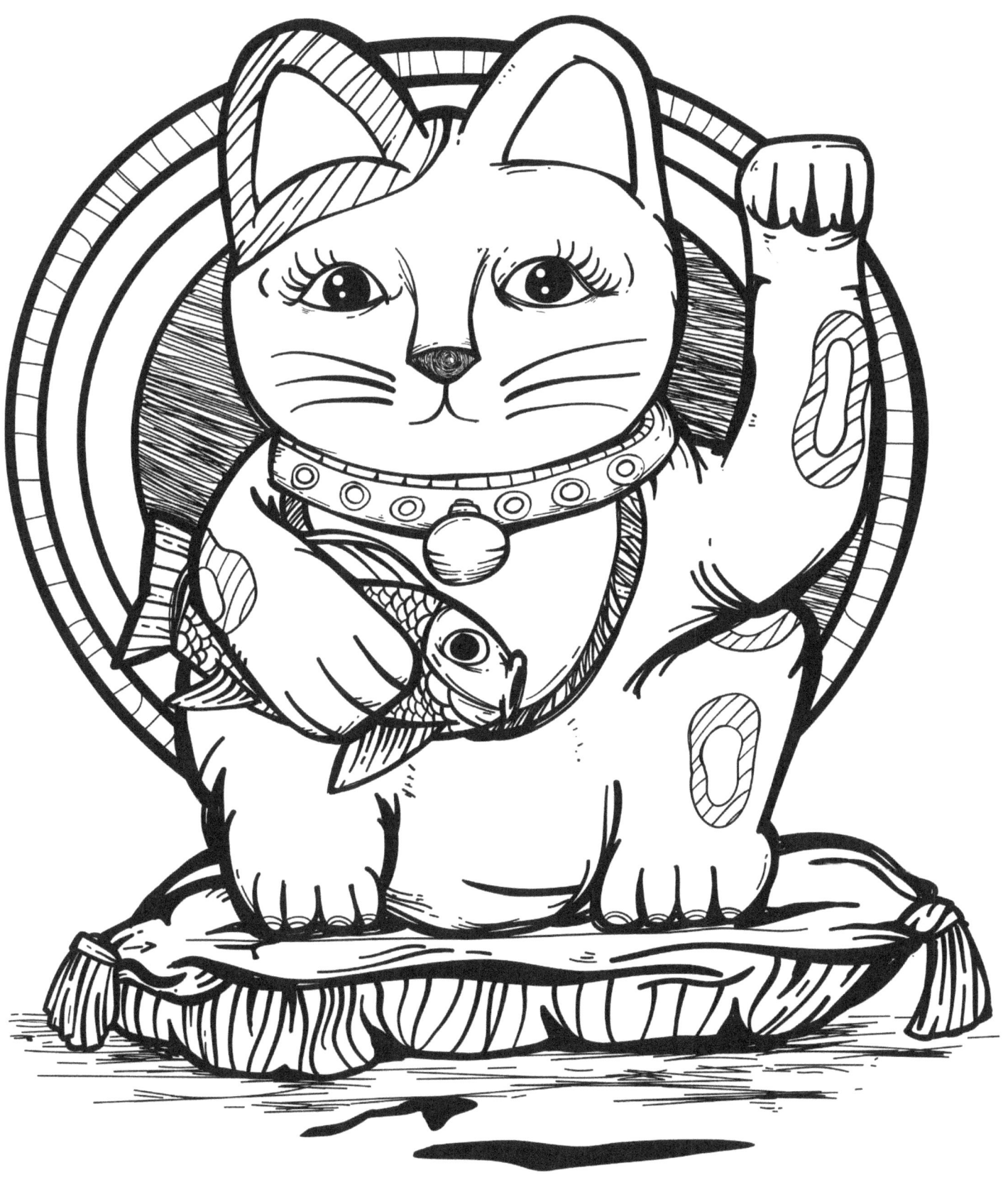

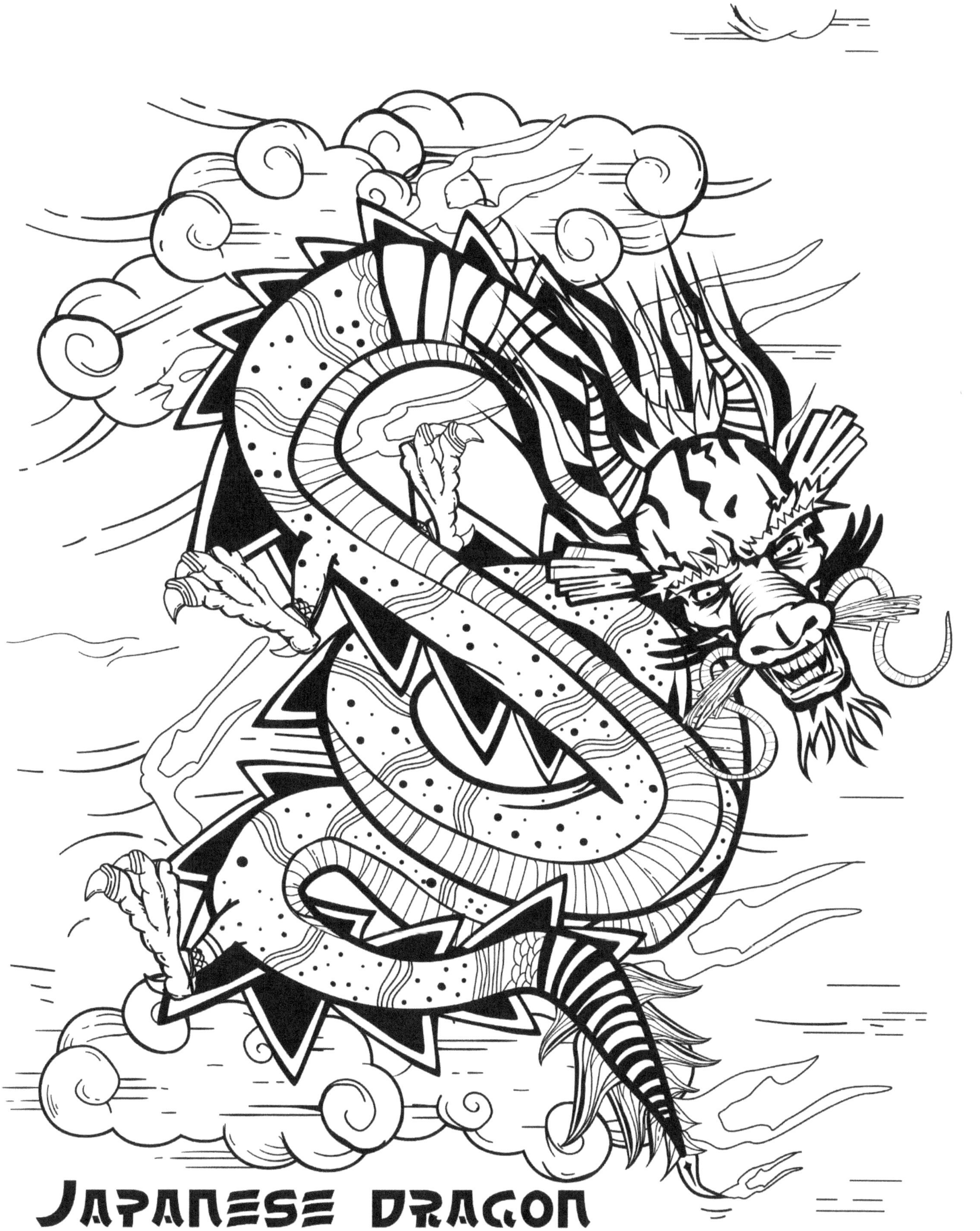

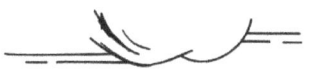

JAPANESE DRAGON

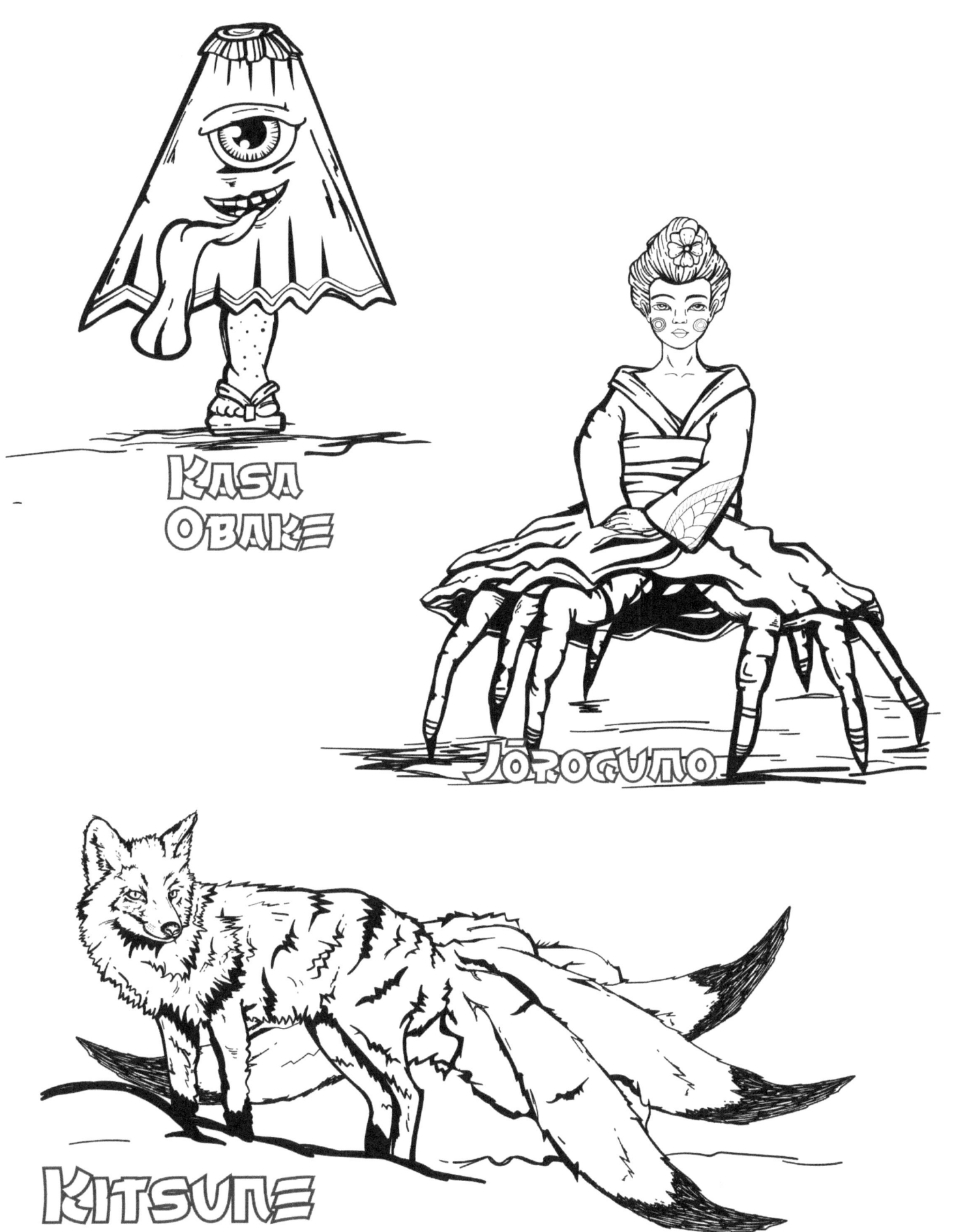

Kasa
Obake

Jorogumo

Kitsune

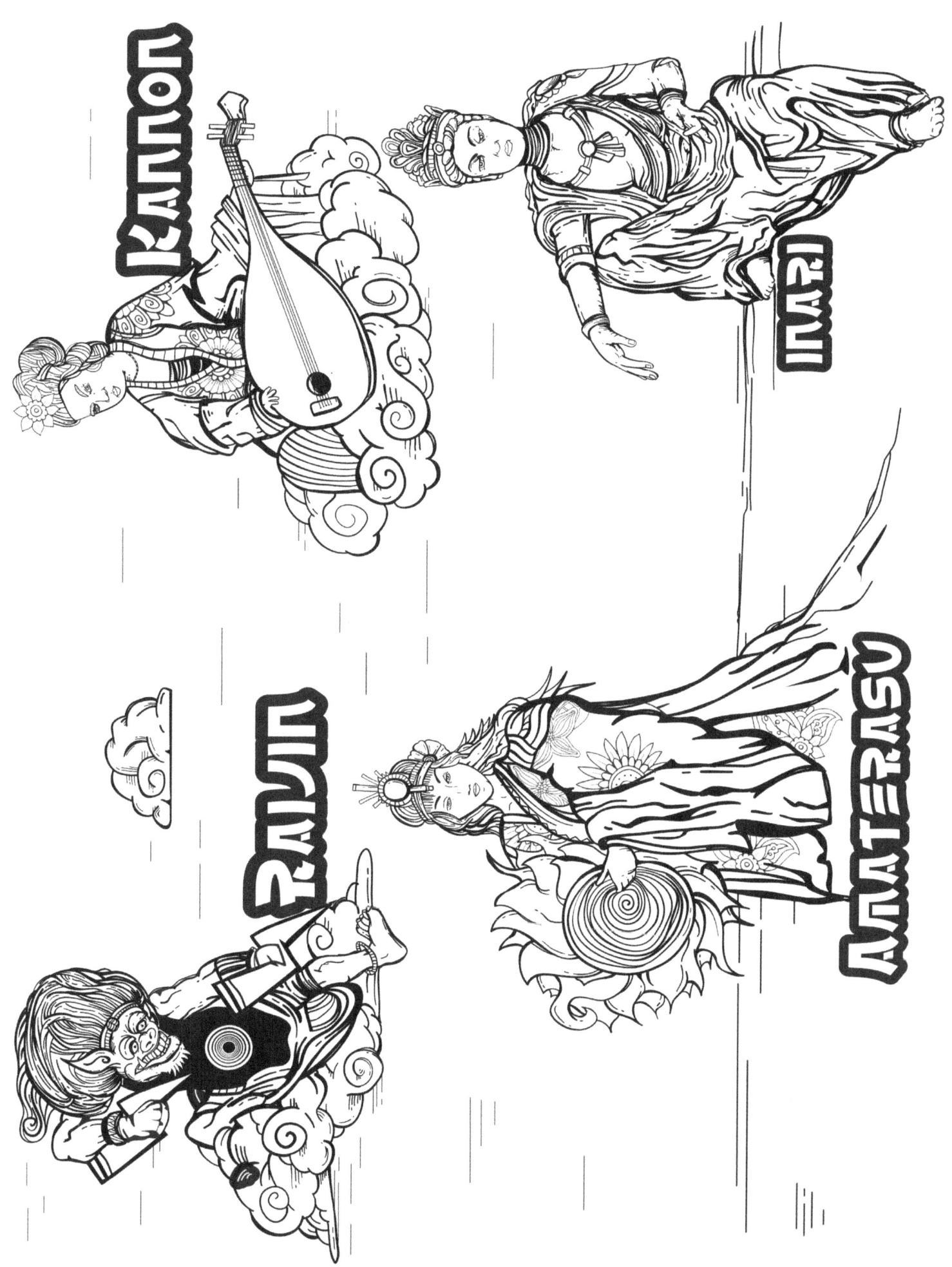

Other Coloring Books from Aryla Publishing

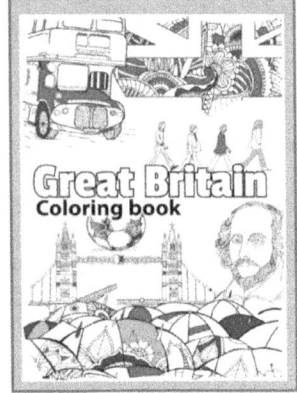
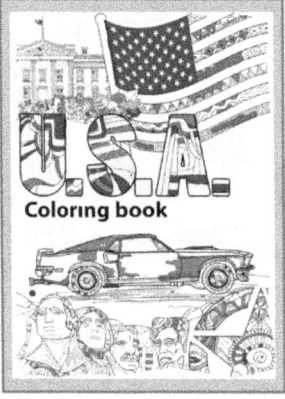
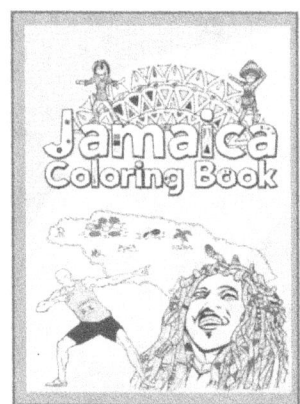
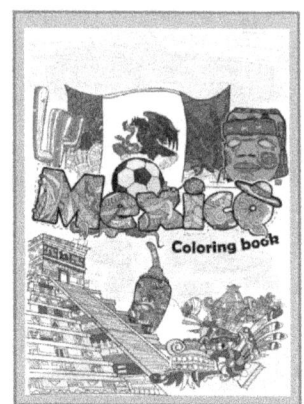

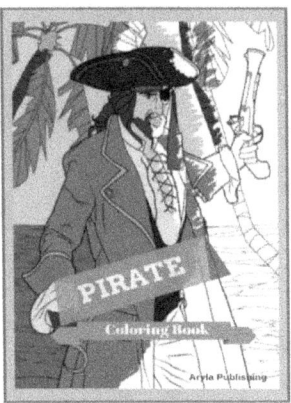
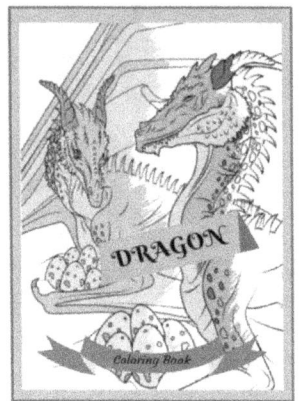
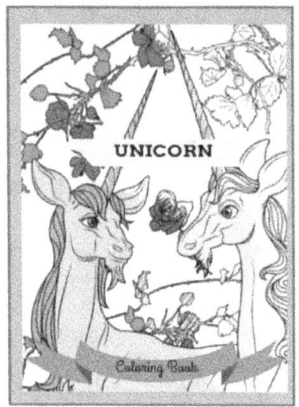
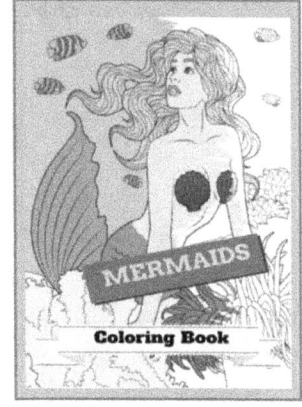

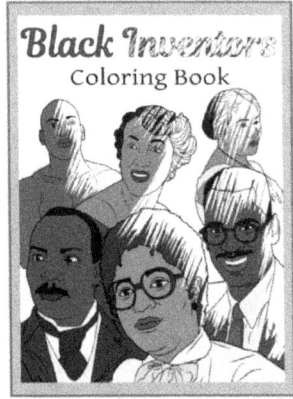
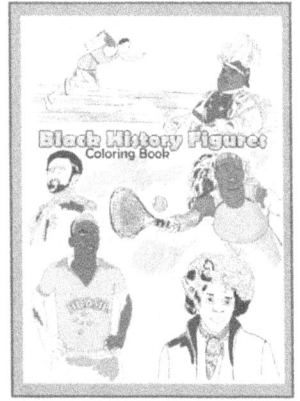
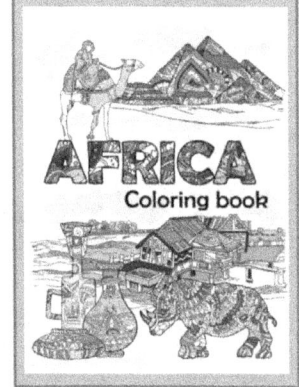
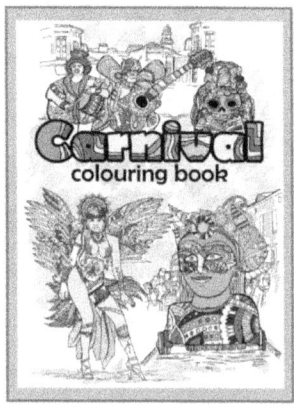

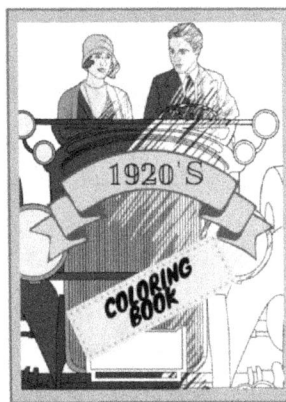
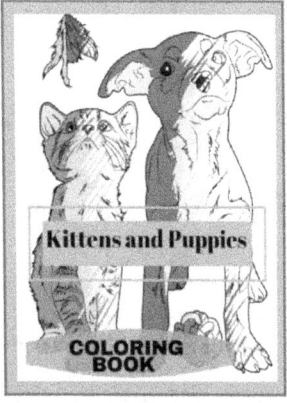
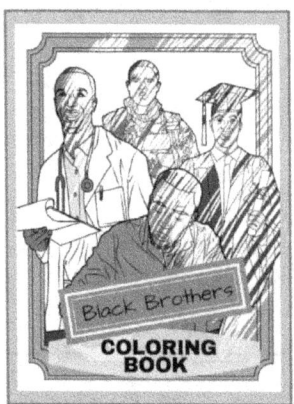
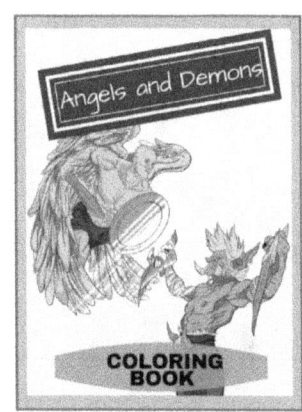

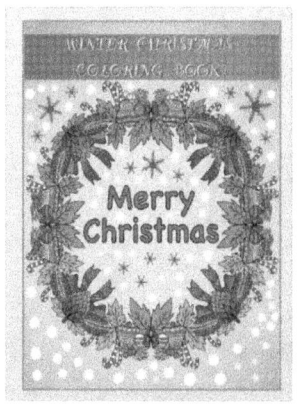

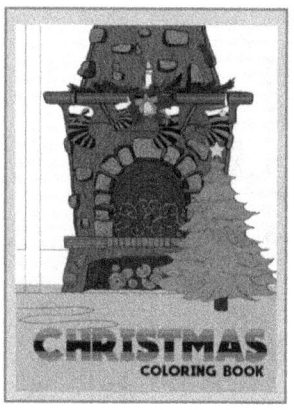
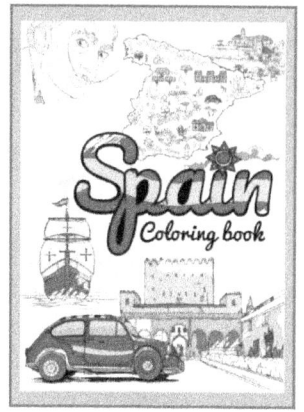
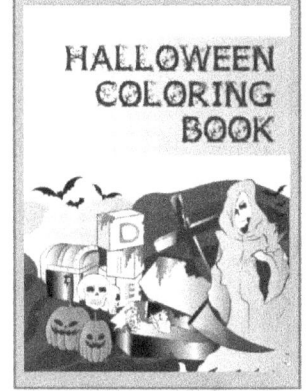
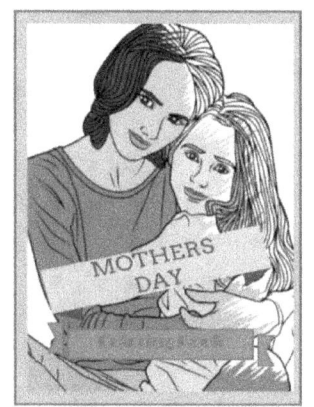
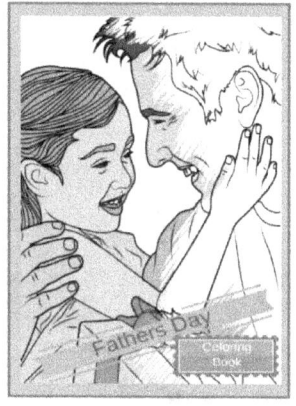
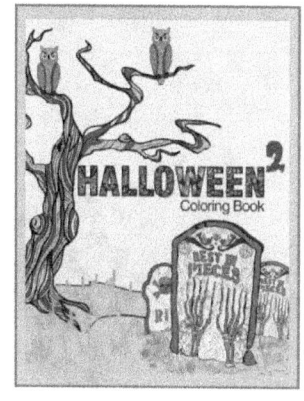
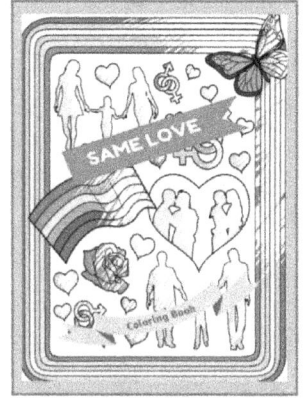
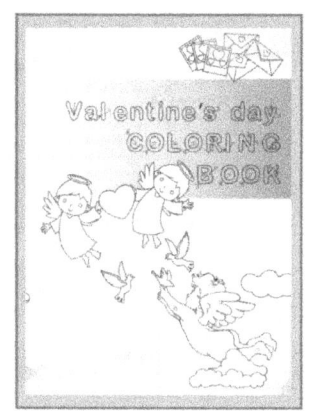
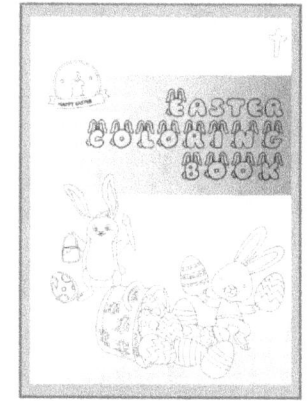
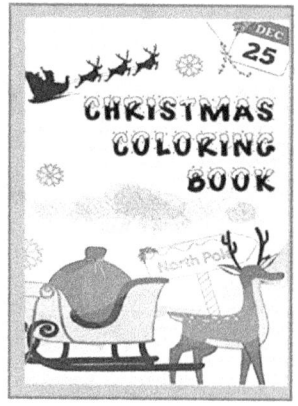
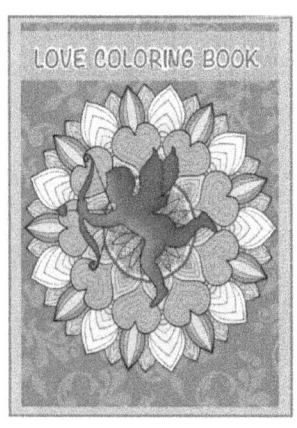
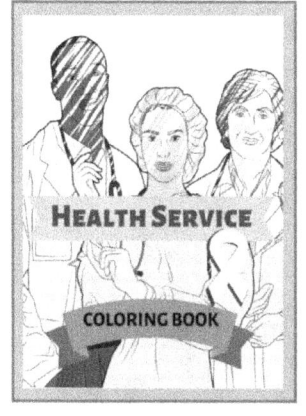
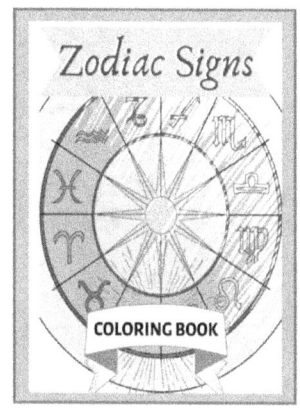
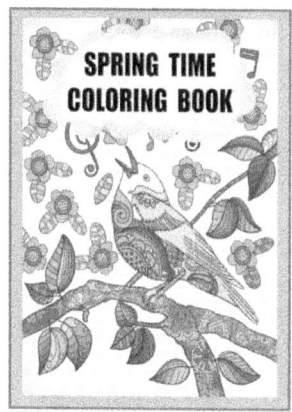

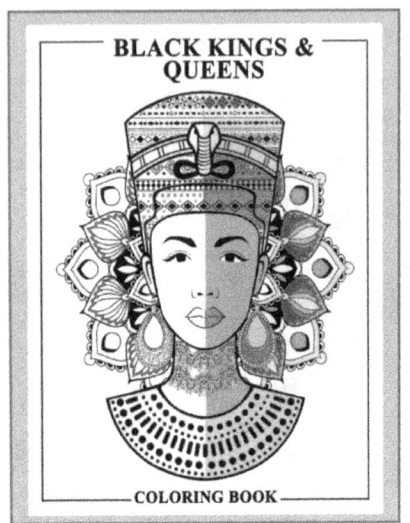

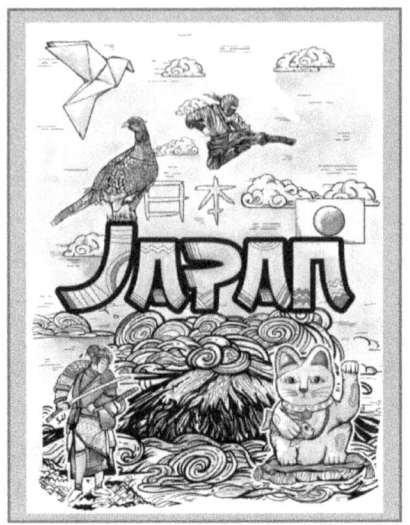

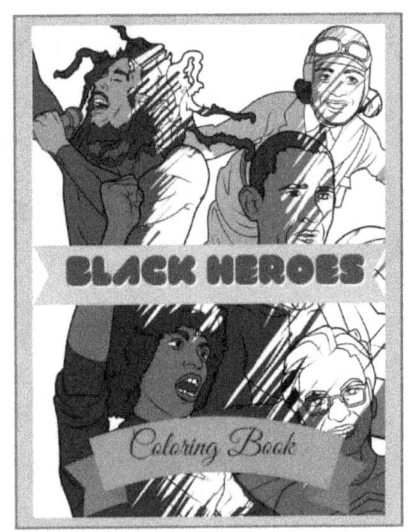

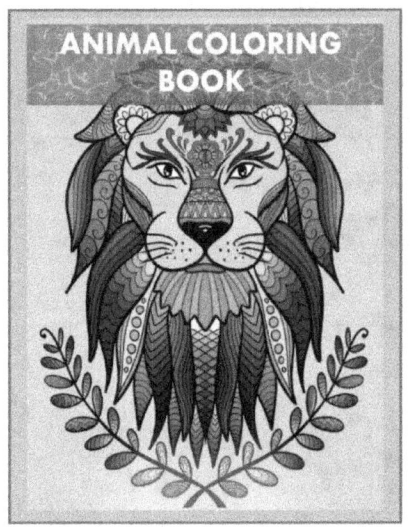

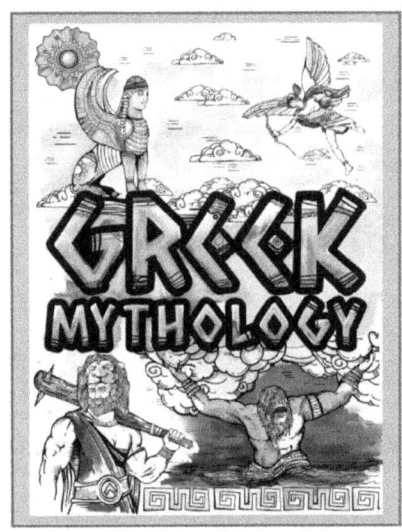

Color In Fun
Kids Books

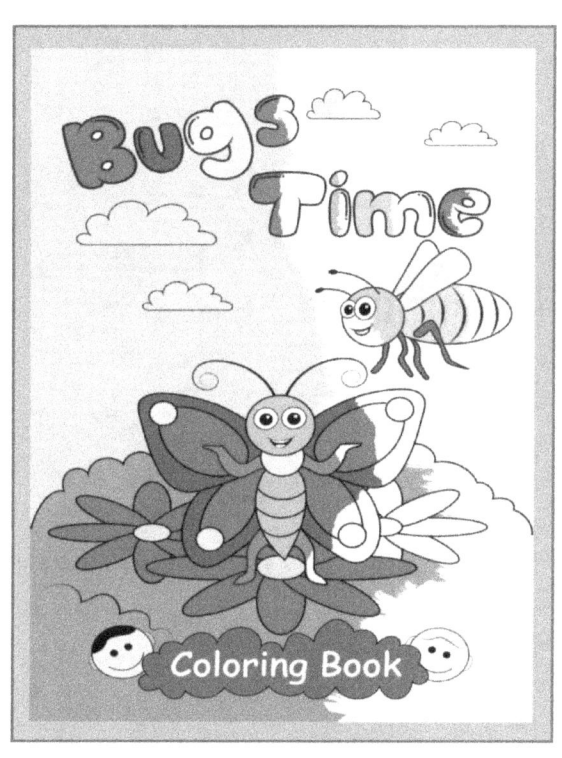

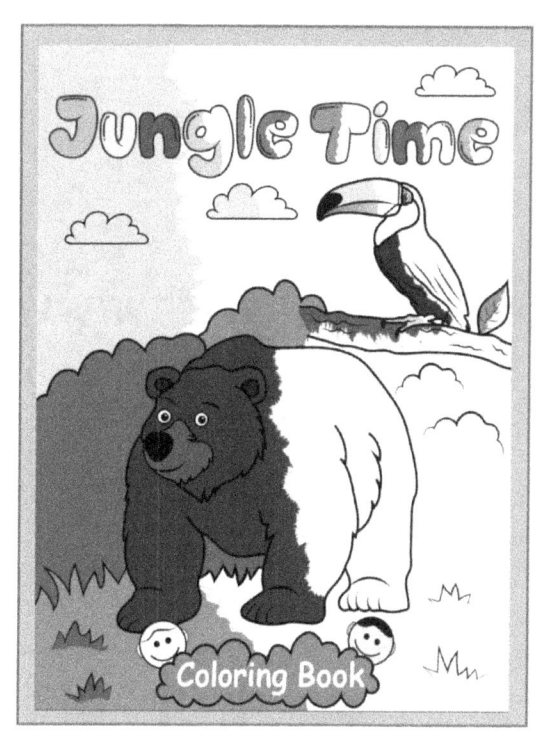

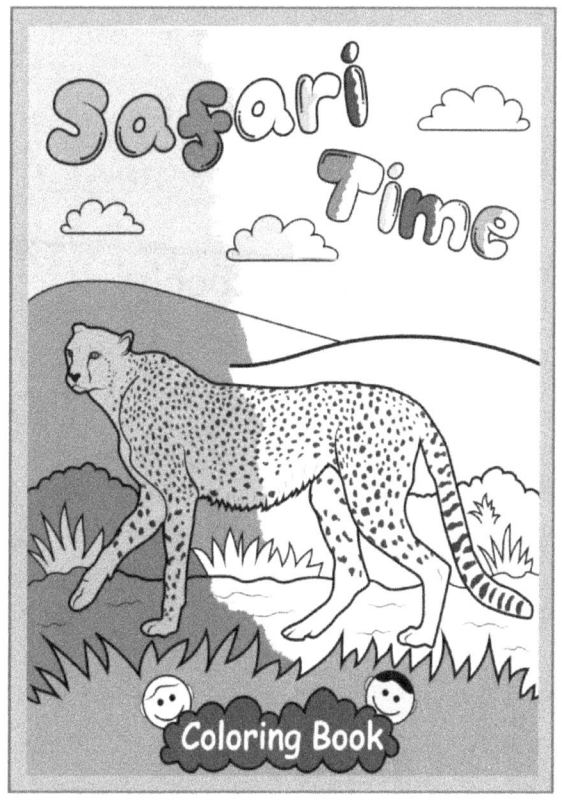

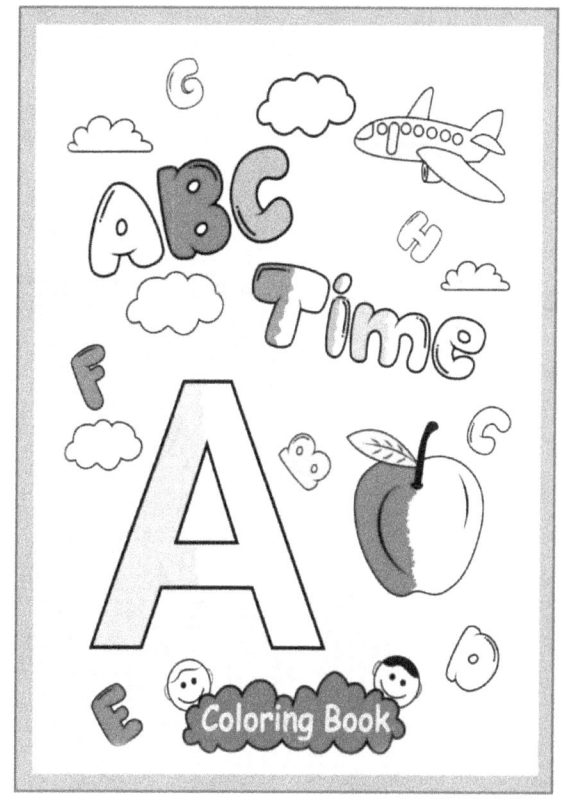

Visit **www.ArylaPublishing.com**
to find out about all new releases.

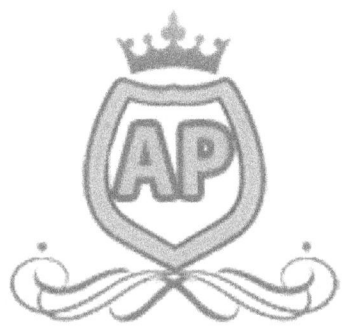

Follow us @arylapublishing on Twitter Instagram & Facebook

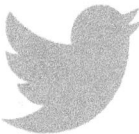  

Search for Aryla Publishing on

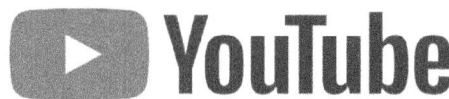 YouTube

Check out our <u>Book Trailers</u>

<u>Subscribe</u> **to keep up to date with new releases!**

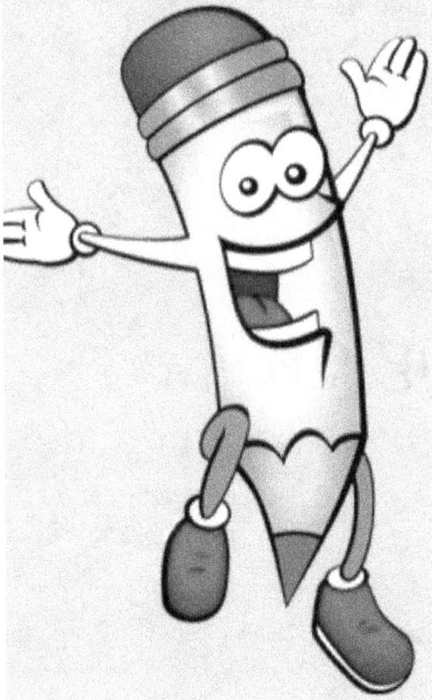

WE WOULD LOVE YOUR FEEDBACK

PLEASE LEAVE REVIEW AT:-

http://bit.ly/japanbookreview